T0260859

97 Things Every Information Security Professional Should Know

Collective Wisdom from the Experts

Christina Morillo

Beijing · Boston · Farnham · Sebastopol · Tokyo

97 Things Every Information Security Professional Should Know
by Christina Morillo

Published by O'Reilly Media, Inc., 1005 Gravenstein Highway North, Sebastopol, CA 95472.

O'Reilly books may be purchased for educational, business, or sales promotional use. Online editions are also available for most titles (*http://oreilly.com*). For more information, contact our corporate/institutional sales department: 800-998-9938 or *corporate@oreilly.com*.

Acquisitions Editor: Mary Preap	**Indexer:** nSight Editorial Services
Development Editor: Angela Rufino	**Interior Designer:** David Futato
Production Editor: Caitlin Ghegan	**Cover Designer:** Karen Montgomery
Copyeditor: Charles Roumeliotis	**Illustrator:** Kate Dullea
Proofreader: nSight Editorial Services	

September 2021: First Edition

Revision History for the First Edition
2021-09-14: First Release
2021-10-15: Second Release

See *http://oreilly.com/catalog/errata.csp?isbn=9781098101398* for release details.

The O'Reilly logo is a registered trademark of O'Reilly Media, Inc. *97 Things Every Information Security Professional Should Know*, the cover image, and related trade dress are trademarks of O'Reilly Media, Inc.

978-1-098-10139-8

[LSI]

Table of Contents

Preface.. xiii

1. Continuously Learn to Protect Tomorrow's
   Technology... 1
   Alyssa Columbus

2. Fight in Cyber like the Military Fights in the Physical..... 3
   Andrew Harris

3. Three Major Planes.. 6
   Andrew Harris

4. InfoSec Professionals Need to Know Operational
   Resilience.. 9
   Ann Johnson

5. Taking Control of Your Own Journey...................... 11
   Antoine Middleton

6. Security, Privacy, and Messy Data Webs: Taking
   Back Control in Third-Party Environments................ 13
   Ben Brook

7. Every Information Security Problem Boils Down to
   One Thing.. 15
   Ben Smith

8. And in This Corner, It's Security Versus the Business!... 17

    Ben Smith

9. Don't Overlook Prior Art from Other Industries.......... 19

    Ben Smith

10. Powerful Metrics Always Lose to Poor
    Communication.. 21

    Ben Smith

11. "No" May Not Be a Strategic Word....................... 23

    Brian Gibbs

12. Keep People at the Center of Your Work................. 25

    Camille Stewart

13. Take a Beat: Thinking Like a Firefighter for Better
    Incident Response.. 27

    Catherine J. Ullman

14. A Diverse Path to Better Security Professionals.......... 29

    Catherine J. Ullman

15. It's Not About the Tools.................................... 31

    Chase Pettet

16. Four Things to Know About Cybersecurity............... 33

    Chloé Messdaghi

17. Vetting Resources and Having Patience when
    Learning Information Security Topics.................... 36

    Christina Lang

18. Focus on the What and the Why First, Not the Tool.... 38

    Christina Morillo

19. Insiders Don't Care for Controls........................... 40

    Damian Finol

20. Identity and Access Management: The Value of User
    Experience... 42
    Dane Bamburry

21. Lessons from Cross-Training in Law...................... 44
    Danny Moules

22. Ransomware... 46
    David McKenzie

23. The Key to Success in Your Cloud Journey Begins
    with the Shared Responsibility Model..................... 48
    Dominique West

24. Why InfoSec Practitioners Need to Know About
    Agile and DevOps.. 50
    Fernando Ike

25. The Business Is Always Right............................. 53
    Frank McGovern

26. Why Choose Linux as Your Secure Operating
    System?... 55
    Gleydson Mazioli da Silva

27. New World, New Rules, Same Principles................... 57
    Guillaume Blaquiere

28. Data Protection: Impact on Software Development..... 59
    Guy Lépine

29. An Introduction to Security in the Cloud................. 62
    Gwyneth Peña-Siguenza

30. Knowing Normal.. 65
    Gyle dela Cruz

31. All Signs Point to a Schism in Cybersecurity............. 67
    Ian Barwise

32. DevSecOps Is Evolving to Drive a Risk-Based Digital Transformation... 69
Idan Plotnik

33. Availability Is a Security Concern Too...................... 71
Jam Leomi

34. Security Is People... 73
James Bore

35. Penetration Testing: Why Can't It Be Like the Movies?!.. 75
Jasmine M. Jackson

36. How Many Ingredients Does It Take to Make an Information Security Professional?......................... 77
Jasmine M. Jackson

37. Understanding Open Source Licensing and Security.... 79
Jeff Luszcz

38. Planning for Incident Response Customer Notifications... 81
JR Aquino

39. Managing Security Alert Fatigue........................... 84
Julie Agnes Sparks

40. Take Advantage of NIST's Resources...................... 86
Karen Scarfone

41. Apply Agile SDLC Methodology to Your Career......... 88
Keirsten Brager

42. Failing Spectacularly... 90
Kelly Shortridge

43. The Solid Impact of Soft Skills............................. 92
Kim Z. Dale

44. What Is Good Cyber Hygiene Within Information
    Security?.. 94
    Lauren Zink

45. Phishing... 96
    Lauren Zink

46. Building a New Security Program........................ 98
    Lauren Zink

47. Using Isolation Zones to Increase Cloud Security....... 100
    Lee Atchison

48. If It's Remembered for You, Forensics Can
    Uncover It.. 103
    Lodrina Cherne

49. Certifications Considered Harmful...................... 105
    Louis Nyffenegger

50. Security Considerations for IoT Device Management.. 107
    Mansi Thakar

51. Lessons Learned: Cybersecurity Road Trip.............. 109
    Mansi Thakar

52. Finding Your Voice...................................... 111
    Maresa Vermulst

53. Best Practices with Vulnerability Management.......... 113
    Mari Galloway

54. Social Engineering....................................... 115
    Marina Ciavatta

55. Stalkerware: When Malware and Domestic Abuse
    Coincide.. 117
    Martijn Grooten

56. Understanding and Exploring Risk........................ 119
    Dr. Meg Layton

57. The Psychology of Incident Response................... 121
    Melanie Ensign

58. Priorities and Ethics/Morality........................... 123
    Michael Weber

59. DevSecOps: Continuous Security Has Come to Stay... 125
    Michelle Ribeiro

60. Cloud Security: A 5,000 Mile View from the Top........ 128
    Michelle Taggart

61. Balancing the Risk and Productivity of Browser
    Extensions... 130
    Mike Mackintosh

62. Technical Project Ideas Towards Learning Web
    Application Security....................................... 132
    Ming Chow

63. Monitoring: You Can't Defend Against What You
    Don't See.. 134
    Mitch B. Parker

64. Documentation Matters................................... 136
    Najla Lindsay

65. The Dirty Truth Behind Breaking into Cybersecurity... 137
    Naomi Buckwalter

66. Cloud Security... 139
    Nathan Chung

67. Empathy and Change...................................... 141
    Nick Gordon

68. Information Security Ever After.......................... 143
    Nicole Dorsett

69. Don't Check It In!.. 145
    Patrick Schiess

70. Threat Modeling for SIEM Alerts........................ 147
    Phil Swaim

71. Security Incident Response and Career Longevity..... 149
    Priscilla Li

72. Incident Management..................................... 151
    Quiessence Phillips

73. Structure over Chaos..................................... 153
    Rob Newby

74. CWE Top 25 Most Dangerous Software Weaknesses.. 155
    Rushi Purohit

75. Threat Hunting Based on Machine Learning............. 157
    Saju Thomas Paul and Harshvardhan Parmar

76. Get In Where You Fit In.................................. 159
    Sallie Newton

77. Look Inside and See What Can Be....................... 161
    Sam Denard

78. DevOps for InfoSec Professionals....................... 164
    Sasha Rosenbaum

79. Get Familiar with R&R (Risk and Resilience)............. 167
    Shinesa Cambric

80. Password Management................................... 169
    Siggi Bjarnason

81. Let's Go Phishing.. 171
    Siggi Bjarnason

82. Vulnerability Management................................. 173
    Siggi Bjarnason

83. Reduce Insider Risk Through Employee
    Empowerment.. 175
    Stacey Champagne

84. Fitting Certifications into Your Career Path............. 178
    Steven Becker

85. Phishing Reporting Is the Best Detection................. 180
    Steven Becker

86. Know Your Data... 182
    Steve Taylor

87. Don't Let the Cybersecurity Talent Shortage Leave
    Your Firm Vulnerable...................................... 184
    Tim Maliyil

88. Comfortable Versus Confident............................ 186
    Tkay Rice

89. Some Thoughts on PKI.................................... 188
    Tarah Wheeler

90. What Is a Security Champion?............................ 190
    Travis F. Felder

91. Risk Management in Information Security................ 193
    Trevor Bryant

92. Risk, 2FA, MFA, It's All Just Authentication! Isn't It?... 195
    Unique Glover

93. Things I Wish I Knew Before Getting into
    Cybersecurity.. 197
    Valentina Palacin

94. Research Is Not Just for Paper Writing................. 199
    Vanessa Redman

95. The Security Practitioner................................. 201
    Wayne A. Howell Jr.

96. Threat Intelligence in Two Steps....................... 203
    Xena Olsen

97. Maintaining Compliance and Information Security
    with Blue Team Assistance.............................. 205
    Yasmin Schlegel

    Contributors... 207

    Index.. 241

    About the Editor.. 248

Preface

An information security professional or "InfoSec Pro" is responsible for protecting IT infrastructure including but not limited to devices, networks, software, and applications. InfoSec Pros are trained to find exploitable weaknesses and fix any potential issues to mitigate and minimize the risk of an attack.

However, the information security field is vast, and navigating a career as someone new or looking to explore other opportunities in the space can feel daunting and uncertain. From understanding enterprise operations, security engineering, and the cloud, to learning how to navigate the number of situations or blockers—these are some of the things you will encounter throughout your career in this industry.

When I was approached to create this book, I envisioned a guide full of practical and actionable advice to better help practitioners navigate the space. Whether you are curious and entry-level or have decades of experience, this book intends to help guide you through your journey by providing practical and technical knowledge you can put into practice starting today. It contains a collection of articles from a global set of information security practitioners, and provides readers with the best practices on solving shared security issues, valuable advice for navigating careers within this industry, and tools needed to solve everyday problems.

We hope that this book will help you better understand and put to practice:

- How to get started, whether you are new to the space or want to pivot into a different path within Information Security.
- How to assess an organization's security posture, and build and scale an Information Security team and program.

- How to understand and implement security and risk management controls.
- How to effectively communicate the importance of Information Security to C-level executives and more.

This book was born, written, and edited in 2020-2021, during a global pandemic. I am deeply grateful to everyone who contributed during a very challenging time. I would personally like to thank each contributing author for sharing their expertise, wisdom, and time. I also want to thank everyone at O'Reilly for making this possible.

My goal is that the articles in this book help you in your career day to day and continue to inspire you to ask questions, challenge assumptions, remain curious, and navigate the journey with ease and grace.

I hope you enjoy it!

O'Reilly Online Learning

 For more than 40 years, *O'Reilly Media* has provided technology and business training, knowledge, and insight to help companies succeed.

Our unique network of experts and innovators share their knowledge and expertise through books, articles, and our online learning platform. O'Reilly's online learning platform gives you on-demand access to live training courses, in-depth learning paths, interactive coding environments, and a vast collection of text and video from O'Reilly and 200+ other publishers. For more information, visit *http://oreilly.com*.

How to Contact Us

Please address comments and questions concerning this book to the publisher:

O'Reilly Media, Inc.
1005 Gravenstein Highway North
Sebastopol, CA 95472
800-998-9938 (in the United States or Canada)
707-829-0515 (international or local)
707-829-0104 (fax)

We have a web page for this book, where we list errata, examples, and any additional information. You can access this page at *https://oreil.ly/97ThingsInfoSecPro.*

Email *bookquestions@oreilly.com* to comment or ask technical questions about this book.

For news and information about our books and courses, visit http:// oreilly.com.

Find us on Facebook: *http://facebook.com/oreilly*

Follow us on Twitter: *http://twitter.com/oreillymedia*

Watch us on YouTube: *http://youtube.com/oreillymedia*

Continuously Learn to Protect Tomorrow's Technology

Alyssa Columbus

The exponentially increasing volume and variety of data being generated today is proving to be an unequivocal target for cyberattackers who see great value in destabilizing enterprise and national ecosystems to create political chaos and drive financial gain.

The SolarWinds hack successfully penetrated the executable files of a leading network monitoring system and is a stark example of the future of cyberattacks. To thwart future attacks at this level of sophistication, change management and ongoing education are needed at a professional level. Personal responsibility and ownership of staying current in information security on the latest vulnerabilities and exposures and with the latest technologies aren't optional anymore. What's needed is a framework for continual self-improvement. I have provided the foundations of a framework that has worked for me here:

Learn with a community.
I've personally found that I've developed new and existing skills much faster (by a magnitude of months) when I've joined a community of learners than when I was trying to learn the same skills alone. By attending local and online user groups, conferences, and other events, you can discover new concepts, hone new skills, and network with possible future colleagues. Also, in a community, you will gain a more holistic perspective of information security and a more complete picture of how others are managing successful information security programs.

Learn the fundamentals of effective communication.
Although an emphasis is often placed on learning the technical skills necessary to succeed in information security, you also need to bring a similar level of intensity to improving your communication skills.

Understanding how to secure a network or be in compliance with a privacy regulation is just as important as understanding how to communicate reports on these technical responsibilities to diverse audiences. Information security is a shared responsibility among every member of an organization, so the real impact of an information security professional's work depends on how well other people can understand their reports and make informed decisions to improve their security program.

Learn concepts hands-on, as it's the best way to grow and progress your information security skills.

Participating in a CTF (capture the flag) or completing a basic project (e.g., securing a WiFi router) for a relative or friend and writing about your experience is often much better than only reading through abstract concepts in textbooks or certification exam study guides. Your experience using real-world tools is just as necessary as your experience studying for academic credentials and certifications, as it translates theoretical ideas into practical outcomes.

Learn how to ask the right questions.

By far, the most challenging aspect of any profession to learn is the intuition for what questions there are to ask and which questions you should ask. The more experience you have and the more you engage your intellectual curiosity, the easier it will be to ask the right questions. Developing information security literacy, or knowing how to find the answers to these questions, can be achieved through risk assessment and mitigation education and practice.

By following this framework, you will be able to not only keep up with the most up-to-date information and protect against the most advanced current threats, but you will also have an enhanced ability to protect against future threats facing tomorrow's technology.

Fight in Cyber like the Military Fights in the Physical

Andrew Harris

I started my career in the US Department of Defense as a cybersecurity engineer, ending my stint there as the Chief for Strategic Programs. The more I saw the department operating what they call Computer Network Defense (CND), fighting in cyberspace, the more overlap I saw in how they were fighting in the other domains—land, air, water, and now space. It became evident that the same approach the military has used in the physical world should be applied in the cyber one.

The OODA Loop

What I'm referring to is the OODA loop—or the "Observe-Orient-Decide-Act" loop. This was made famous by US Air Force Colonel John Boyd (*https://oreil.ly/9hARx*).

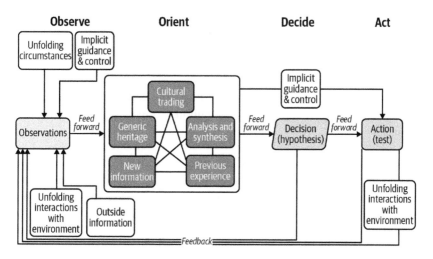

To summarize the concept, the goal is to properly synthesize data and accurately respond to it, faster than your opponent. The last bit is equally important.

How does this relate to cybersecurity? When thinking of responding to cybersecurity incidents and breaches, and within the context of what I call the "Iceberg Effect," one needs to discover all observables an adversary has, containing and responding. However, this is rarely ever a one-loop effort.

This activity happens multiple times, enabling cybersecurity professionals to *confidently* respond to and evict an adversary. For that reason, it's the feedback loop from one loop into the next loop that is of operational importance.

Prior to performing the first loop, one should ask themselves what feedback they need to see if they've been successful. Has the adversary attempted to break out of containment strategies added in the first loop? Has an asset previously unknown to be compromised shown evidence of a previously discovered indicator of compromise (IoC)? After you disabled a compromised user, did you see activity from it elsewhere?

Having this high-level strategy is paramount when strategizing, acquiring products, and operating any product or tool in a production environment, against determined and capable adversaries.

Containment Helps to Prevent and Inform

Earlier we referenced *containment* plus the fact that a mission or series of operations is rarely a one-OODA-loop operation. There is a cat-and-mouse game to worry about when responding to any cyber incident.

Containment is necessary for two reasons:

1. It prevents the adversary, once detected, from achieving its goals or further escalating.
2. It informs later OODA loops. By setting these containment strategies up, any attempt of breaching the containment model becomes a signal in itself.

Containment can be resetting or disabling an account. If you do this, any attempt to use the specific account again should be immediately investigated —it potentially could be the adversary attempting to use the account, even on a computer you previously had no idea they had access to.

Containment could be separating the identity or control plane (see Three Major Planes, page 6) where the adversary was discovered from the rest of the network. This sometimes causes pain, but when fighting a real adversary, it's a necessary step to confidently evict them. This could be performed a few different ways, including segregating accounts, disabling network traffic, forcing a choke point through a firewall (think software-defined networks or SDNs), and so on. Once implemented, all attempts to break this new technical control should be reviewed in the following OODA.

Three Major Planes

Andrew Harris

The world is evolving fast. The iPhone first came out in 2007, starting what many call the mobile device movement. The Chrome browser from Google was introduced in 2008, reigniting browser wars. Cloud service providers have emerged as one of the largest growing markets in technology, changing how developers meet the needs of their end users and how enterprises across the globe meet their business requirements. Data is no longer purely "on-premises," requiring virtual private network (VPN) connections; end users expect to be productive anywhere at any time.

This just scratches the surface on major changes cybersecurity professionals have had to wrap their minds around. How do security experts react as fast as their business needs, without blindly trying to slow everyone down?

What I have found tremendously helpful is breaking things down into three major planes or buckets. They are:

- Data
- Identity
- Privileges

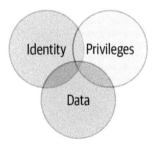

Understanding these three planes, at their fundamental level, we can define higher-level abstractions, including what others call the "control plane" and "access plane." Unfortunately, there are three major flaws we see even experienced professionals make when facing challenges, preventing them from seeing the fundamental challenges:

1. Not focusing enough on where these planes *meet*
2. Confusing or merging the concepts of Identity and Privileges
3. Not applying the hypothetical syllogism

Not Focusing on Where the Planes Meet

Looking at each plane by itself is boring. It's also not effective. When looking at data for example, one must think about *who* can access that data. The *who* here is the Identity plane. The *how* is *the privilege* that identity is granted that allows them to access the data. This is a drastically oversimplified example, but many don't break down the problem as such.

Identity Versus Privileges

Let's use Microsoft's Active Directory as an example to describe where two planes, Identity and Privileges, meet. It's easy to believe that "Enterprise Admins" are *the* administrators of an Active Directory environment. However, it's also true that a security group is explicitly given the permissions *locally*. By default, it is given the necessary privileges to manage everything else—but nothing is stopping from changing that!

This group is given no extra permissions on other "domain-joined" computers. If someone in the Enterprise Admins security group logged on to their Windows device, nothing by default gives them any local administrator privileges. Context is king.

What does this mean?

This means a malicious actor can take another identity and give it Enterprise Admins–like privileges, without ever modifying the Enterprise Admins group. All too often, security teams try to secure a particular security group without auditing the privileges that make that group special! Are there other groups who also have the same privileges? If so, are we explicitly aware of these additions?

In addition, this means if an adversary compromises an identity on a device that isn't "privileged"—or not an administrator—it doesn't mean the identity doesn't have privileges *anywhere*; context is key!

Not Applying Hypothetical Syllogism

Anyone who completed fourth-grade logic has learned this—rarely are they given the name, however. Many know it as this:

- First premise: A → B
- Second premise: B → C
- Conclusion: If A, then C.

Remember that Active Directory example? If an identity owns Active Directory, and Active Directory controls *domain-joined* computers, what can we conclude? Even though that Enterprise Admin's identity doesn't have permissions explicitly on the local Windows computer, it *can* control Active Directory. Therefore, for the Active Directory boundary—all computers who've joined the Forest—these identities in Enterprise Admins are critical to secure!

Notice the word *boundary*? The security of this boundary is built around protecting that identity, and equally important, the privileges that give it the permissions.

Wrapping It Up

Don't get lost in a single plane. Focus on these overlapping parts of the planes. Regardless of how technology continues to evolve, these planes will always exist—data, identity, and privileges. Their implementation and trust relationships may change, but the core concept of discovering these and using that information to defend the environment will always be paramount.

InfoSec Professionals Need to Know Operational Resilience

Ann Johnson

Cyber breaches happen, and bad actors are becoming increasingly more sophisticated and persistent in their approaches with tactics, techniques, and procedures (TTP). As organizations struggle to keep up with both the sophistication and volume of attacks by implementing new tools, processes, and human capabilities, one thing that often gets lost is the need to recover quickly from a cyber event and keep your critical business systems online to avoid further brand or financial loss.

There are steps an organization can take to make certain they are operationally resilient by ensuring they are cyber resilient. I am not going to focus on technology here, but rather process and people.

First, it is essential you identify, classify, and properly protect your critical business systems. One of the first things that organizations must do is properly identify where their critical business systems and business data sits, and put in place the proper controls around these systems and data.

Second, it is essential you have a plan, and you test that plan. Similar to an organization's existing plan for any type of natural or human disaster, you must prepare and test a plan for a cyber disaster. And you must inform and transparently communicate with every employee, from executives to your most junior team members, to think of a cyber disaster in the same way you think about a natural or man-made disaster. This communication should be continual, and you need to find the ways to make it interesting and relevant to your team, based on the culture of your organization.

Third, you need to publish the plan, and the plan must be comprehensive. You cannot just lay out technology controls and a plan to recover the systems; you must also include human resources, public relations, legal, finance, the executive staff, employee communications, the board of directors, shareholders, and the public. How, when, and what you communicate is essential to minimizing and mitigating damage to the brand of the company —short and long term.

Fourth, you need to test the plan. It is critical for you to lead tabletop exercises, at least twice per year, to make certain your entire staff has clarity around their role in the event of a major cyberattack. You need to document roles and responsibilities as well as clearly communicate expectations. You need to model everything from the most basic scenarios to the most extreme scenarios. We have witnessed companies that failed to plan and were subject to significant financial loss and brand impact. Contemplate whether you will need third-party help—technical, legal, communications—and contract that help in advance. Think about it as having a disaster recovery team on retainer.

Finally, you must continually update and edit your plan, based on market dynamics, changes in method of attack, growth/change of your own organization, and what you learned from past events. Take the best practices from any crisis your company has endured and apply them to cyber events.

Any organization is vulnerable to a cyberattack. There is no perfect security. We continue to witness an increase in the willingness of the most sophisticated actors to expend significant funds and resources to attack targeted organizations. Your ability to quickly recover and continue business operations could make the difference between the ultimate success or failure of your organization.

Taking Control of Your Own Journey

Antoine Middleton

Earlier in my career, I struggled in many roles because I waited for someone to guide me through the wildness of information technology. My expectation was that if I showed up willing to learn, I would be taught by others. In hindsight, this was never the case and very naive of me. In reality, I had to become proficient at doing research, improving my soft skills, learning the unpopular processes, and excelling at the fundamentals.

You may think this sounds great, but it certainly requires an enormous amount of effort, sacrifice, and persistence to be successful. So what does this look like in practice? At one organization I worked for, I intentionally asked for access to the development environments and deployed every job-related tool possible. I saw this as my playground to learn, make mistakes, and grow. I was able to learn to code in Python using this method by expanding the internal toolset capabilities. This is not an overnight change. Consistency is the key. The shift to the cloud has also leveled the playing field in IT. Each cloud platform offers a free tier to gain the necessary experience whether currently employed or looking to gain employment. *Taking control of your own career journey is one of the most powerful things you can do.*

"The greats are the greatest because of their excellence in the fundamentals."

Have you ever experienced being in the room with those IT "superstars"? Do you question whether or not you can be like them? Despite the many posts, newsletters, or social media commentary, no one individual has all the answers. Truth be told, many of them and those same people that work beside you have no idea as well. Yet they are afraid to ask for help or ask questions and give the appearance of not knowing. In my opinion, nothing gets done effectively or efficiently in isolated environments, so ask questions and learn daily the foundational principles. Also, network with others to create a community of like-minded individuals to hold you and them accountable for growth.

I'm reminded of a story about a music store owner who stocked shelves in a particular order to force the consumer to ask for help in finding what they were looking for. I thought that was excellent. Human connections! I relate this to my experience working in DevSecOps. I was a part of a company that failed an audit, and stress levels increased due to limited or no effective communication between the various departments. Communication is always a vital foundational principle, especially in InfoSec. The most difficult security engineer role for me to succeed in was not due to the technical nature of the role but noncommunicative individuals.

One of the greatest "tools" I've gained working with other internal departments is to be flexible. Sure, I could easily say we can't do that because of security requirements or principles, but what does that lead to? Departments doing shadow IT. Enjoy a little gray as everything is not black and white with technology. Being flexible has helped me to be involved in projects early and advise on security best practices before becoming a checkbox.

So, to summarize how to take control of your journey or TL;DR:

1. Do research.
2. Take advantage of free opportunities.
3. Become great at the fundamentals and build up from there.
4. Be an effective communicator.
5. Be flexible.

This will work in InfoSec and in life.

Security, Privacy, and Messy Data Webs: Taking Back Control in Third-Party Environments

Ben Brook

One of the most common challenges for InfoSec professionals is the lack of visibility into the security and data protection practices of third-party ecosystems, including those owned by partners and vendors. Core business functions like marketing, HR, sales, customer service, finance, and even engineering teams increasingly use third-party software to run daily operations. Reclaiming security in a messy and poorly linked system requires new tools.

Today, the average company uses more than 200 software as a service (SaaS) vendors.[1] Too often, the onus is put on legal colleagues to develop contracts and liability clauses that offer paper promises instead of true, deep, and technical system checks we can audit and log. Contracts and policies can't guarantee technical execution, and words are not engineers.

The framework below is one way to approach managing privacy across data silos when you don't have full control of the environment.

Establish Technical Visibility

1. *Understand who has what.* Until there is a way to do this at the code level, leveraging vendor assessments in your procurement process is a solid starting point to identify who has access to which systems and data. Depending on your organization's risk posture and tolerance, you may

---

1 "2020 Annual SaaS Trends—Blissfully Report" (*https://oreil.ly/oHJkE*). *Blissfully,* October 23, 2019 (*https://oreil.ly/f2sdN*).

also decide to require vendors to produce third-party audited compliance certifications like SOC II or ISO 27001 reports.

2. *Prioritize properties based on potential risk* with a few key questions: Does the vendor process personal data? How does your team authenticate into the third-party system? Does the vendor offer granular access control or is everyone an administrator? Are there any flags on their security assessment? What are the vendor's compliance certifications? How do they comply and enable you to comply with privacy regulations? In which region are they processing the information and does it constitute an international transfer?

Exercise Technical Stewardship

There are two areas to exercise technical management: data in transit and data at rest:

1. *Data in transit*, i.e., flowing to the vendor system: On the data pipeline to the vendor, it's important to have a control surface that you manage. This allows you to monitor the data flowing into that system, and gives you a way to shut off the valve.

2. *Data at rest*: Modern privacy laws require companies to operate on personal data when a user makes a privacy choice. To do this, you must be able to download, update, and delete personal data in vendor systems. For medium-sized or larger organizations, this should be done programmatically with a hub-and-spoke model. The hub is often encoded in Kafka as a producer with consumer processes (spokes) built for each system. With this architecture, you can set up consumer processes (such as serverless functions) that will run your API integration code for deletion in vendor environments such as Salesforce, Google Ads, etc. Some small businesses may be able to manage this manually if they have a low volume of user requests.

The rise in SaaS and the lack of visibility into third-party vendors means lucidity and stewardship are critical for all InfoSec professionals responsible for protecting sensitive user data.

Every Information Security Problem Boils Down to One Thing

Ben Smith

It's the dirty little secret of our industry: just about every challenge that we face in trying to secure our infrastructure from threats ultimately comes down to an asset management problem.

In many organizations, asset management is viewed as pure drudgery and a never-ending stretch to accomplish. Assets residing on your network, not just those dedicated to your employees but perhaps your supporting third parties as well, are not static entities. Today's asset inventory is almost guaranteed to look a little different than yesterday's. Much like Sisyphus pushing the boulder *almost* to the top of the mountain every day, your asset management goal posts can and will change daily.

Yet if you don't know *what* is plugged into your network, if you don't know *who* is plugged into your network, your visibility will be dangerously limited, along with the ability to do your job in securing your organization.

Further complicating this task: defining exactly what an "asset" is may not be a totally straightforward exercise. In some cases, assets to be protected by you and your team may not be limited to traditional server, endpoint, or network gear. Are we talking about everything with an IP address? Is a digital signing certificate an asset that should be cataloged and protected like a physical device? Should identities and their associated entitlements be included as assets to be tracked and managed? Is some or all of the intellectual property for your line of business an asset in and of itself? Take the time to formally define what "it" is. You can't protect it if you haven't defined what it is.

Without comprehensive visibility across your assets, without knowing if one device is "more important" than another, you are almost certainly wasting time and resources when incidents are captured and reported. You want your first-level security operations analyst to recognize immediately if this incident is a first-tier problem (for example, something affecting a domain controller, an executive's laptop, or a dedicated network connection to an essential business partner), or some other, lower-priority tier. This single data point around asset criticality can dramatically improve the life of that overworked analyst by making it very clear how they should prioritize today's ever-growing list of incidents to be worked.

Even organizations who are tight and reasonably current on this asset management question can be thrown for a loop when a merger or acquisition arrives. If you're on the acquiring side of a transaction, be thinking about how soon you, the information security professional, will gain access and visibility into the "new" organization. In the absence of a clear understanding of the incoming assets, do you keep the two environments largely separate for an extended time? What due diligence do you need to complete before these two environments are fully connected and even combined? In a perfect world, information security will be represented *prior* to the transaction closing—you want to be in there as early as practicable.

Make the time to get to know your network and everything connected to it, before the bad guys do. If your adversary is the first person to comprehensively map out your infrastructure, you are in for a very rough ride.

And in This Corner, It's Security Versus the Business!

Ben Smith

Too many promising careers are derailed by the belief that working in information security is purely a technical job.

Many of us arrive into the information security space via the technical realm. Perhaps you got started through hands-on configuration of firewalls and routers, or managing your organization's domain server, or developing secure interfaces to databases, or working an IT help desk where you kept raising your hand when someone called in with a security question. Or all of the above.

And as your knowledge expands, along with your career, you may even move up within your organization: from a frontline engineer or analyst, to a network architect, to a team lead, to a people manager. Each step up the ladder tends to expose you to a wider set of technologies and responsibilities.

At some point during all this upward mobility, a light bulb switches on. Some of us notice it, but many do not.

Every organization grows silos over time, partitioning corporate functions into separate management buckets. It's expected, and largely natural, but over time the presence of these silos can be unhealthy—even a threat to your organization's ability to scale your business.

Nowhere is this threat more pronounced than in an organization where the information security team is unaware, or unwilling, to take the time to understand the needs of the business. It's sometimes easy to forget that you are ultimately employed to support the business. You can't view yourself only as an investigator or an enforcer.

You are part of "the business," whether it feels that way or not. And, as an information security professional, if you don't understand how your department fits into the broader goals and charter of your organization, you're doing a disservice not only to your boss, your team, and your company, but your career as well.

But I think you already know what I'm talking about. More than once, you've commiserated with your information security coworkers about "those people" who just don't get it. "Can you believe that marketing set up their own web server?" "Why don't our executives appreciate why we need to secure that data?" "Yeah, she just walked out of here with that laptop. I don't think her boss understands it's much more than simply theft of a device."

Far too frequently, what's happening here is that different languages are being spoken. It's like an English speaker and a German speaker attempting to communicate with one another—each speaker may divine a hint of what the other is saying, but both ultimately are speaking past each other. And when that happens, there is no communication at all, only noise.

Security and the business don't have to have an adversarial relationship. They should not. They *must* not. Remember, both of these teams are ultimately operating under the same charter: protect and leverage the intellectual property of the organization to maximize revenue and/or delivery of services.

Your job, wearing your information security and risk management hat, is to help educate your business peers: while you and your team bring specific skills and tools to support this charter, it is the business that ultimately owns the risk for any specific project. You can help them achieve their goals, and your goals, at the same time—but only if you know how to speak with one another. It's a partnership!

Be that wise information security resource who takes the time to get to know your peers within the business line(s) you are supporting. Become the key translator in your group who can speak both languages.

Your career will thank you.

Don't Overlook Prior Art from Other Industries

Ben Smith

There's nothing I like better than uncovering a clue that someone else may already have figured out the very problem I am grappling with. This is especially awesome when that potential solution arrives from a completely unexpected source, someplace well outside the boundary of information security.

Here are some examples in thinking about how you might deal with...

Adversaries

We tend to be hardwired in thinking that "telecommunications" is a recent innovation. But communicating at a distance, and the networks humans use to move a thought from one place to another, have taken many forms over the centuries. Think about Depression-era bicycle couriers on Wall Street, commercial express companies, national postal service programs, semaphores, flag signaling, line-of-sight and relay communication, heliographs, fire-based beacons, smoke signals, synchronous optical telegraphs, and carrier pigeons.

Do you suppose there might be (already learned!) lessons about how each of these telecommunications networks was exploited for mischief or crime, poisoned with false data, or simply used in some unanticipated way?

Projects

As an information security professional, your coworkers may consider you an unwelcome representative from the Department of No. Where this can become especially uncomfortable is when we are tasked with contributing to projects headed by other departments. When you are asked to weigh in on one facet touching your world, how do you tactfully make your point and get it to stick?

Enter the world of improvisational acting. Improv can be leveraged as a means to communicate more productively, especially around tough asks from your colleagues that set off your internal information security alarm bells. The key to any successful improv session is to keep the conversation, and the ideas, flowing by answering "Yes, and…" (accepting) instead of "No way!" (blocking). Agreeing to consider a request, while at the same time laying out how you might fulfill it, is usually more productive than turning someone down immediately. Hint: this is an essential skill upwardly mobile information security professionals tend to figure out early on.

Coworkers

Security awareness programs usually fall under the purview of the information security team. Why do some security awareness programs fail? Bland content, poorly aligned objectives, and settling for a one-time checkbox compliance approach can all contribute to short- and long-term failure. A common thread across many successful security awareness programs is the goal to not just make end users aware of potential areas of exposure, but to actually change underlying behaviors that are contributing to the problem.

Broadening the conversation to encourage basic hygiene and instill new foundational habits are appropriate goals not only for information security, but in fact you may recognize these very same concepts and language from the world of public health risk management. Are there takeaways from prior public health initiatives that we can apply to our security awareness efforts today?

And a final point, important enough to break out on its own here: *Ask your family. Ask your friends.* Just because they aren't immersed in your information security world doesn't mean they can't offer up a story, or an analogy, from their perspective that might just help you with your problem *du jour*. Ask them what they think about your challenge.

Even better, this phone-a-friend approach forces you to be able to describe your challenge clearly and cleanly to someone not already in the thick of it. If you can't do that, then perhaps you don't fully understand the nature of the problem.

Don't jump to solve a challenge without first taking the time to think about adjacent industries, or related problems, or possible lessons from history.

Or more succinctly: don't reinvent the wheel.

Powerful Metrics Always Lose to Poor Communication

Ben Smith

It's a big day!

You recently were promoted into a leadership position within information security, and next week you get to shine a light on some of the great work you and your team have been doing: your first-ever presentation to your VP, your upstream C-level executive, or perhaps even your board.

You think you've done your homework. You know all about the tools installed throughout your environment, and you're eager to explain how each tool snaps into your broader vision of how to protect the organization.

Perhaps most importantly, you've spent a lot of time sourcing compelling metrics you will present to your audience—pulling them from your current operational reports, as well as from the standardized reports provided by many of your vendors. You're thinking you want to take this opportunity to demonstrate all the ways that the technology you interact with daily protects the organization.

And yet, when you walk out of your presentation, you'll realize that you missed the mark. What happened?

The most common failure point: you created your metrics and your accompanying presentation before considering your audience. Too many of us in the technology world get wrapped up in creating the perfect metric(s) to demonstrate how effective we are in our jobs. But are those the metrics your audience needs to hear about? More importantly, are those the metrics your audience wants to hear about?

Knowing your audience, understanding what *their* goals are out of your metrics presentation, before you even step into the room, is often overlooked as a basic preparation step. While you were pulling together your content, did you bother to check in with the one person in the executive audience whom you know the best, and ask him or her for feedback on the metrics you planned to bring to the presentation? The world's "best" metrics from your perspective may not be, from the perspective of someone higher in the organization.

If you think your board is interested in hearing about the quantity of dropped packets at the firewall, or the amount of incoming spam that was identified, or the number of failed logins across your organization, you are wrong. Like the weather, these metrics largely reflect events you have no control over.

A quick way to gauge the effectiveness and actionability of your metric: if it doesn't pass the "so what?" test, that is a sign you still have some work to do.

Or perhaps your metrics and your storyline were spot-on, but your delivery was not. Standing up to present confidently in front of a group of executives is a skill. Translating technical content to a nontechnical audience is a skill. Telling a story that meets both your goals and the needs of your audience is a skill. Lining up the right metrics, in the right order, to support your budget ask is a skill.

And the good news is that these skills can be sharpened and improved over time—with practice. Leverage a trusted colleague ahead of your live-fire exercise—and you get bonus points if that colleague is outside your department, someone who may bring an alternative point of view. Devoting some talk time, and a bit of your report space, to a taxonomy that briefly defines a handful of the key terms you plan to use can pay dividends for your current conversation as well as those in the future.

Do your homework ahead of time. Don't settle for merely reporting the weather conditions. Define, gather, and present metrics that will move your audience towards whatever goal you bring to the meeting.

"No" May Not Be a Strategic Word

Brian Gibbs

No. It is the easy way out, so delete it from your vocabulary.

As an information security professional, you generally are working for someone in an organization. The simplistic goal of an organization is to make a profit. Your role is to help that organization to understand and accept risk. There is a concept around balance where you can be 100% secure and 0% functional or 0% secure and 100% functional. Helping the organization find the correct balance is your role.

How do you go about saying no? *You simply do not start with no.* If you are in senior leadership, ask to schedule a meeting to review the idea or item in more detail. Then ask probing questions around this idea or item. You may surprise yourself with the additional information you gather. The initial no reaction may start to fade away with ideas on making this more secure and enabling the organization to proceed forward in a safe and secure method. Even if you still "feel" the answer is no, you should document the risks and present them back; if the organization decides to accept the risk, that is fine. You did your part by establishing the known risks and learning more about the idea or item without saying NO!

If you are a more junior member of the team, you can assist as requests come in by applying similar processes. It never hurts to pick up the phone or schedule a quick meeting (even 15 minutes) to ask more probing questions. You may have assumptions about the request, and learning more may open new ideas on how to solve the request to reduce the organization's risk. It may be necessary to escalate to someone who has liability within the organization. The concept of liability is someone who has a financial stake at risk. The person(s) that may accept risk may be a board of directors, CXO, or even a VP. Depending on your organization's policies, they generally can accept liability. The process also assists with you not being the person who says,

NO! Your role was to review the risk and help guide so that a liable person accepted your organization's right level of risk.

When all else fails, give it a 72-hour rule when your initial reaction is NO. Take those other meetings, do the additional research, and help profile the organization's overall risk. If after the 72 hours have passed and it is still NO, proceed to present your findings. Taking the emotion out of the process will elevate you higher within the organization and help you gain more respect.

In closing, consider the organization's purpose. How will this new product, idea, or process impact the risk profile and profit of the business? Does this drive forward with the mission of the organization? Help be the enabler and be known as a partner to the organization, not the person that says NO and is known as the blocker.

Keep People at the Center of Your Work

Camille Stewart

People are at the center of information security challenges. I'm sure you've heard "people are the weakest link in security" multiple times. That thinking is counterproductive. Most cyberattacks rely on social engineering or exploiting human psychology to gain access to buildings, systems, or data. And one of the most important tools in preventing cyberattacks is encouraging user adoption of proper cyber hygiene and security tools. This makes clear that the actions of people are at the core of the challenges and the solutions, which is why understanding the user and meeting them where they are is foundational to better security outcomes. A traditional technology-centered approach limits you to making decisions based on the threat rather than also contemplating how behavior changes the attack and the response.

The central question no matter your role in information security is, "Why do people behave the way they do?" Identity, lived experience, culture, community, societal norms, and a number of other factors all play into how an individual or institution behaves, i.e., how they use technology, perceive risk, and adopt security and privacy mitigations. Technology is used within a society by people who introduce personal perspective and inevitably bias of all kinds into its creation, adoption, implementation, and use. That is basic human psychology. Therefore, as an information security practitioner the technical and policy mitigations you implement to combat information security threats need to account for the human element, which includes recognizing how cognitive bias may be impacting your decision making.

Cognitive bias is "a strong, preconceived notion of someone or something, based on information we have, perceive to have, or lack. These preconceptions are mental shortcuts the human brain produces to expedite information processing—to quickly help it make sense of what it is seeing."[1] A human-centered approach to information security augments a technology- or threat-centered approach by looking at how data and systems are accessed, how technology is used in context, and how to recognize where cognitive bias influences decision making. Attackers continue to weaponize the ever-increasing wealth of personal data and social justice challenges like racism, sexism, and bigotry against us to perpetuate attacks and advance malicious ends. Not to mention that malicious actors don't discriminate. They build diverse teams, are from different backgrounds than yours, and are motivated to exploit every human weakness. To combat that, information security professionals must leverage the benefit of diverse perspectives and focus on the people at the center of the challenges. Human-centered information security requires:

Continuous review of the societal context
Understanding the societal and cultural nuances of technology use and access is integral to building policies and technical solutions that secure systems, serve people, and encourage the right behavior.

Centering culture on accepting and understanding all people
Constantly audit the perception of information security to better understand which cognitive biases are impacting the organization and how. This accountability is important and starts by continuous cultivation of a company culture rooted in intentional diversity, inclusion, and equity.

Creating tools and processes to mitigate bias
One potential tool is to create an equity review board that holds the team accountable to mitigate bias in its work as well as constantly seek to understand the user.

Critical thinking skills
Implement training that promotes the development and exercise of analytical, communication, and problem-solving skills. This reinforces the creativity and open-mindedness necessary to outwit attackers, mitigate inevitable bias, and adapt to the evolving threat landscape.

Keeping people at the center of the work and seeking to meet them where they are is essential to effective information security. Don't lose that awareness!

---

1 "How to Identify Cognitive Bias: 12 Examples of Cognitive Bias," *MasterClass*, November 8, 2020 (*https://oreil.ly/Vp38V*).

Take a Beat: Thinking Like a Firefighter for Better Incident Response

Catherine J. Ullman

The security world is full of dumpster fires these days. Unfortunately, incident response doesn't come naturally to an operational mindset where the focus tends to be on reactive problem solving. As a volunteer firefighter for over twenty years, and an incident responder for more than half of that time, I've learned a lot about what is and isn't effective in each. There are surprising parallels between fighting real-life fires and the firefighting that passes for today's incident response. Let's consider two: the need for patience and the importance of avoiding tunnel vision.

First, let's discuss the need for patience. Striking a balance between swift response and patient reflection is often the difference between life and death, in a very literal sense for the firefighter and a figurative sense for the security professional. There's a strong temptation to want to jump right in when someone yells, "Fire!" What I've learned, however, is that patience really can be the key to a successful incident response, just as in the fire service. As much as firefighters weigh the risks involved in their plan of attack, incident responders need to do the same.

Taking a beat—one moment to think through your approach—can be the difference between success and failure. During that pause take the time to observe whether there are any life safety risks, which could be anything from asbestos or flooding in a server room to a tangle of electrical wires. Also, consider that it is possible that what you're walking into isn't actually a true incident, despite the urgency of the request that brought you there. Ask yourself what the real risks are of the situation in question and assess the potential implications of the actions you are considering. Patience will also improve your capacity for attention to detail both in your own observations and what you are being told.

Next, let us discuss the ramifications of tunnel vision. Getting caught focusing on the wrong areas can cost precious time. Firefighters are taught to initially pull their trucks up just past a structure fire in order to view at least three sides of the building so they understand the challenge they face. As soon as possible, an officer is responsible for doing a 360 of the property in order to understand the full scope of the incident. Using this methodology they can avoid situations like focusing on flames blowing out the front door only to later discover victims in hidden basement apartments that are only visible from the rear of the structure.

Incident responders should follow a similar thought process. Do not necessarily assume that everything you are being told about the incident is accurate or even relevant. Thoroughly document all the information you are given and then verify what you've been told against your own observations. For example, you might be told that you are being called in to deal with a case of ransomware. Instead, could it be the case that it is just a single phishing message? Depending on the credentials involved, a single phishing message could be far less damaging than ransomware and require far fewer resources to investigate.

Even though threats surround security professionals like a burning ring of fire, thinking like an actual firefighter can help make your investigations more effective and efficient. Be sure to take a step back and take a 360 of the situation. Take that beat and think before jumping into an incident. Patience and contemplation of the bigger picture will help you avoid getting singed and ultimately make you a better incident responder.

A Diverse Path to Better Security Professionals

Catherine J. Ullman

Like many InfoSec professionals of my generation, my background is not in computer science. I wound up in my first technical support role after discovering that my original, nontechnical career path was unsuitable for me. A good friend suggested I explore technology. Twenty years later I find myself firmly entrenched in the security field. In retrospect, a letter of recommendation from a former supervisor containing the statement, "Cathy is very good with computers" was very telling. As a result, I would argue that there is no specific path one should take to get into computer security. What matters more is obtaining some key skills on that journey, which are not necessarily technical in nature. Let us explore them now.

First, communication skills are essential for success in this field. Security professionals, whether entry level or advanced, are often asked to explain technical ideas to people who are not technical. Furthermore, it is not uncommon to be asked to communicate ideas to people at different levels within an organization. The ability to express one's thoughts effectively and efficiently, either while speaking or in writing, is a must. Effective communication involves listening (or reading carefully), not just speaking/writing. This step provides feedback so that both parties know whether they are being understood. Patience is key. Efficient communication means choosing one's words carefully, based on what must be conveyed. Frame the conversation for the audience; i.e., focus on what matters to them and speak/write to them at a level they can understand and relate to. In particular, avoid acronyms and "geek speak" when communicating with non-IT people. The more you learn about technology in this field, the easier it is to take for granted what you know that others do not.

A second fundamental skill for being an effective security professional is the desire to learn combined with tenacity. Security is an ever-changing field, which is in part of what can make it exciting as well as challenging. Having the desire to learn and the tenacity to obtain the required knowledge can be especially useful for obtaining a particular technical skill set, but can also be useful in nontechnical situations. Being willing to jump directly into a challenge until one not only completely understands the problem at hand, but follows it through until it is solved, is crucial.

Finally, and perhaps most importantly, all good security people must exhibit compassion and empathy. Because all aspects of security involve encouraging positive behavioral change, security should be seen as a people problem more than one of technology. In order to properly motivate this change in someone, it is critical to understand both where they are coming from and what is important to them. Furthermore, having empathy and compassion for everyone helps remove the "us versus them" mentality, allowing security to be seen as part of the solution organization-wide, rather than an impediment.

Information security is an enormous field, encompassing many different areas such as governance risk and compliance, security operations, and training and awareness. Although some of these areas require significant technical abilities, not all roles do. What they do seem to have in common, however, is a need for strong communication skills, a desire to learn coupled with tenacity, as well as compassion and empathy. Whatever path one takes to obtain these skills is the right one. Companies produce the best products when they are innovative, and innovation comes from the diversity of its teams. Security teams are no exception. Thus, focusing on these skills, rather than people coming through a particular path, just might uproot two weeds with one pull.

It's Not About the Tools

Chase Pettet

It is demanding feeling responsible for the safety of someone else's data. Especially when catastrophe is on the near horizon. In order to pursue effective mitigation, we need to communicate to our business the need for response before loss is realized. Arm flailing, chest puffing, and pantomiming are rarely enough to adequately spur the need for proactive resourcing and action. This communication impasse informs a disconnect of purpose that permeates interactions between security professionals and the business. A near miss with the knowledge that our ability to avert the next larger threat is missing can be a dreadful outcome.

In these situations, the practice of information security can feel like a perfunctory corporate mascot of mutually lost faith. This state of ineffectual influence is paved with the perception that the purpose of a security program is to protect the business from itself. This sense is cultivated by feature factory security programs focused primarily on the implementation of technical capabilities and divorced from the ends of the business as a whole. Often the business has imposed this dysfunction by encouraging a security model of last-mile interventions outside of the adopted software development life cycle. While this seemingly allows internal teams to remain naive to the risks their opportunities are married to, it does so by creating a false sense of due diligence. On the security side, this model establishes a poisonous accumulation of tactical decisions that are out of touch with the actual risk appetite of the business. The remedy is framing security as a top-down driven strategic initiative and risk-informing component within the business.

Securing information as a practice is a function of risk management, and as in all risk management there are polarities to be managed. This polarity of risk and opportunity is the arena that all businesses and thus all security programs are beholden to. There is a saying: "The only secure network is the one that's turned off." This is recognition of the ultimate trade-off at our disposal, and the futility of expecting any mitigation strategy, short of avoidance, to be completely successful.

As there are no infallible strategies, communication and readiness are the key differentiators for a successful information security program. Effective communication propels the business to make the most informed decisions in pursuit of its objectives. As risk is meaningful in relation to objectives, reflection on the mindset of security as an afterthought demands we examine the premise that we can achieve them without ensuring the safety of our assets as a first-class concern.

Business leaders must adopt risk, threat, vulnerability, likelihood, and impact as shared and required language for success in an information-driven economy. Security professionals must adopt quantitative expressions of risk that have a common denominator for the business in financial impact. This is how trust is built that extends across business objectives, strategic security spending, and the tactical expression of that strategy in execution and prioritization.

Risk management is a storied and deep subject of study. The modern evolutions, as they relate to information risk, seem to have been carried over from the banking and financial industries over the course of the last twenty years. This integrative approach is what is required of both security professionals who seek to be successful as part of a larger organization, and organizations who seek to bring an effective security posture to market.

Four Things to Know About Cybersecurity

Chloé Messdaghi

Here are four things to keep in mind about cybersecurity.

Hackers Are Not Attackers

The first is that hackers and attackers are not interchangeable terms for the same thing, i.e., threat actors. They use similar skills but radically different objectives.

A *hacker* is an ethical security researcher who proactively probes and explores an organization's vulnerabilities with the goal of identifying them for the organization before an attacker can exploit them for malicious purposes. Hackers may seek compensation through a vulnerability disclosure program (VDP) or a bug bounty program, or just want to alert an organization to vulnerabilities and then, having allowed time for remediation, and with permission, may publish their research findings.

In contrast, attackers probe an intended victim's network and systems seeking vulnerabilities to exploit—either for monetary gain, or to extract valuable or sensitive data.

In short, hackers serve to protect and are allies. Attackers are anything but.

Vulnerability Disclosure Policies Strengthen Defenses

VDPs are an important tool in strengthening organizational cybersecurity. A disclosure policy is an agreement between an organization and independent security researchers (also known as hackers) that benefits both parties. VDPs invite security researchers to examine an organization's network and systems within a specified scope of exploration, not exploit, and to notify the company of any vulnerabilities found without fear of prosecution or harassment.

It's worth keeping in mind that while most security teams spend their time building defenses, attackers spend theirs probing for weaknesses to exploit. Moreover, security teams must be constantly vigilant and right 100% of the time; attackers need just one lucky finding to hit their goal—the odds are in the attacker's favor.

The foundation of a productive disclosure policy is a four-part promise by the organization. It promises to secure and protect its data; to invite productive, nonpunitive alliances with hackers; to accept alerts about vulnerabilities and quickly address them; and to fairly compensate or otherwise recognize the researcher.

This collaboration lets organizations work with some of the best minds in cybersecurity to strengthen their defenses—a win-win.

Burnout Is a Real Risk

Cybersecurity is a demanding career, and because of the urgency that often surrounds it, professionals can be susceptible to falling into "always on" work modes, which can lead to burnout, a genuine and dangerous health risk that affects concentration and emotional stability, and can greatly degrade quality of life.

The move to working from home (WFH) further increases our susceptibility to burnout, both because the boundaries between work and off-time hours are eroded, and because of reduced communications among team members. Burnout can lead to unchecked vulnerabilities, which can turn into breaches or patches not being tested.

Team leads need to watch closely for signs of burnout, and intervene in positive ways. Ensuring time off, active listening, strengthened communications, and investments in team upskilling are among the best prevention measures.

Upskilling: Professional Growth

Security professionals must constantly face off against bad actors who continually evolve their threats and tactics. Upskilling helps give cybersecurity pros the skills and confidence to meet emerging and evolving challenges, and provides them with tools to further advance their careers.

The best upskilling opportunities are hands-on, gamified, and enjoyable challenges and training. It's an important way to reward and recognize security teams, while equipping them to keep up with the sector's changing demands.

Upskilling also provides important incentives for personnel retention—a clear challenge in cybersecurity. The tools and opportunities for growth are a tangible reward for security pros, and can help demonstrate an organization's commitment to its team's professional development.

Vetting Resources and Having Patience when Learning Information Security Topics

Christina Lang

If you plan on learning tokens, or really anything in information security, *always start out by using only official sources.* I cannot tell you the number of times I have been publicly embarrassed or utterly confused because I used a YouTube video, blog post, or vendor's website to try and learn about authentication, authorization, and tokens when I was first starting out in identity and access management.

The trouble with unofficial methods is that they are often outdated by the time you read or watch them. Or they are opinionated or may not contain entirely accurate depictions of a process. They may also use the wrong terminology or may unintentionally omit helpful pieces of information (such as the difference between a confidential or public client and why that matters when considering what token grant or flow type to use).

I have found, more often than not, that studying the official IETF (Internet Engineering Task Force) documents or the most current publication from OpenID Connect or OWASP (Open Web Application Security Project) to be the best route when trying to learn a topic. Often if the document you are reading has been updated and a more current version is available, they will list that on the document itself so it's clear that the information within the outdated version is no longer applicable or recommended.

Another thing to remember is that Rome was not built overnight, nor will you be capable of learning everything you feel you need to in a short period of time. When I began my journey to becoming a Token and Federated Login Subject Matter Expert (SME), it took me months of study and dedication. It was my full-time job so I was able to dedicate at least eight hours a day to nothing but studying and reading scholarly research articles. However, many people do not have that kind of time available and that is perfectly OK. Pace yourself. Study what you can, when you can, and work at your own pace.

It will be impossible to know everything you feel you "should" know. Part of the beauty of being in information security is the fact that you can usually rely on someone you know to help you find the information you need. Most people understand and accept that we don't know everything in this vast field. It would be like expecting a neurosurgeon to tell you specific details and treatment options on a lung disease. That's not their area of expertise, which is why you go to the expert for that specific problem area.

Not knowing everything does not lessen your credibility by any means. In fact, being honest about what you don't know is often the best thing you can do for yourself when working in information security. It will usually be painfully obvious to others if you aren't well versed in a topic and often won't gain you any favors for stating otherwise.

In the end, be honest, be humble, and accept that it is virtually impossible to know everything in this field, and that is OK. Find what areas might interest you and study the heck out of them!

Focus on the What and the Why First, Not the Tool

Christina Morillo

"If All You Have Is a Hammer, Everything Looks like a Nail"

In information security, we tend to focus on tools at the expense of not understanding what these tools are there to accomplish. By doing so, we miss a deeper level of understanding and problem solving because we snap to specific technologies without a clear understanding of the challenges we need to solve.

Years ago, being a technology practitioner meant that you were tool agnostic. While you may have had more experience with one technology or platform over another, the most critical part was understanding what problem implementing a piece of software, a new tool, or technology was there to solve. The industry has become focused more on shiny new tools and implementing these new technologies before identifying problems, business impact, and requirements.

As an information security professional, be intentional about *understanding the problem*, current processes, and potential impact before purchasing or implementing any new technology/tooling. Deploying the latest and greatest SaaS tool will not solve your organization's core issues. Look beyond.

Understanding the Problem

InfoSec teams are highly reactive—for a good reason—but this can also be detrimental to a team's growth. Many InfoSec teams will rush to purchase a best-of-breed tool: for example, Team Blue will rush to acquire an incident response tool, but it lacks a formal incident response process and an understanding of current state flows. Instead of understanding the problem first, teams jump to purchase and implement *more technical debt* and systems that sit unused for six months. Before you engage any tool vendor for a POC (proof of concept), be proactive and clarify the exact problems you are looking to solve internally. Doing so will require you to converse with stakeholders across the company and solicit feedback. Then, document these requirements along with any organizational expectations, challenges, or possible limitations.

Understanding Current Processes

During your first month at an organization, do you start deploying tools and systems? Probably not, because you still have limited visibility into challenges and opportunities. I cannot emphasize how important it is to focus on the what and the why. Taking this approach will allow you to become proficient in problem solving first and platforms, systems, and tools as a fast follow. Even if you are skilled in specific tooling, every company operates differently, and one size does not fit all. *Take the time to understand short- and long-term needs because your choice of tool may not be what the company needs.*

You Cannot Solve for What You Do Not Understand

Information security is not about the tools, systems, or platforms. It is about mitigating risks and protecting the confidentiality, integrity, and availability of an organization. The tools should help you accomplish that end goal, but only once you truly understand what that is. Your job as an InfoSec practitioner is to understand these gaps and challenges.

Focus on the *what* and the *why* before you jump to deploy yet another tool or service that will ultimately cause more issues.

Insiders Don't Care for Controls

Damian Finol

Putting together security infrastructure and controls around your assets, data, and employees is an insurmountable task. Many CISOs (chief information security officers) go through a shopping list to check out boxes: next-gen firewalls, SIEMs (security information and event management), endpoint management, HSMs/keystores, etc.; they believe that good security means deploying "basic" controls to cover your business against attackers and then calling it a day.

Insiders however, care little for these controls. A firewall? Well, they're already inside your network. Keystores? Useless when they already have access to systems. SIEMs? What if they can become a superuser of that collector? In short, insiders care little for your controls and have everything to gain from taking advantage of the usual InfoSec paradigm of stacking them mainly to prevent external attackers.

Truth be told, external attackers are no different from internal threats once they have gone past your defense systems. Most of the time these attackers either compromise an internal user account, or a role account, and from there, every action they take is within the parameters defined by the organization of what that employee can do. Access sensitive customer data? No problem. Perusing your source code? Not a problem either.

So, the true ant work in InfoSec comes with performing a threat model of the organization within the view of an insider. This means looking at ALL the roles in the org: your C Suite, the folks in marketing, HR, your SREs/DevOps, software devs, customer service reps, and yes, even those contractors that have an account on your identity system.

Take for example, a software developer. They most likely have some level of access to your deployment pipeline, or in the case of machine learning (ML) engineers, to highly sensitive customer data sets. How do you plan for them to iterate on their work while handling sensitive customer data *and* keeping it safe? For most of these, there is no off-the-shelf solution, and the issue requires the creation of a policy that would reduce the risk of an insider exfiltrating data.

In the preceding example, you could create a policy where an ML engineer can work with sensitive data in an ephemeral git branch only after another person has also approved this temporary work (usually a manager). An insider seeking to exfiltrate data would find it harder to exfiltrate a temporary subset that needed validation from a second party to be generated in the first place.

Notice if this same data is accessed by other systems higher in the stack, e.g., your customer support organization. Start with your user data, finding every pathway to it from all angles; in most cases it isn't as simple as looking at your LDAP/AD calls because many systems such as CRMs (customer relationship management) can impersonate or indirectly access this data using a master role account. Then perform a threat model based on the different types of roles that can access this data: your software developers create code that process this data, your site reliability engineers maintain the uptime on it, data scientists give you insight on it, and yes, your usual sales, marketing, and even HR folks need it.

In short, even after you've built a moat around your assets and deployed the best in preventing external attacks, a disgruntled employee or someone with unfettered access getting phished will cause great damage to your organization and make those defenses look like ornaments.

Identity and Access Management: The Value of User Experience

Dane Bamburry

When information security or cybersecurity comes up for discussion, most conversations begin with traditional concepts such as firewalls and intrusion protection, which are usually geared towards a defensive mindset. Identity and access management (IAM) is the cybersecurity domain that forces us to incorporate enablement and user experience into the thought process more so than in other domains. Although IAM has been around for a long time, it has become a more mainstream security topic of discussion in the past 10 years. With the addition of smartphones, connected devices, and an infinite amount of usernames and passwords to keep track of, it is extremely important to understand how to develop an effective strategy as secure access to consumer- and business-centric data has become the cornerstone of information technology.

Some may argue that identity and access management goes back to the introduction to usernames and passwords, but to truly understand this vital component of the cybersecurity landscape, we need to go back and understand what is defined as an identity. A general dictionary description of identity is the proven fact of being who or what a person is. So what makes a person's identity a fact? A birth certificate, driver's license, and passport are a few examples of what helps to identify a person. When they are used to gain access to some location/facility (e.g., airplane for a flight), after the document has been verified as official and belonging to the person presenting it, a successful IAM transaction has occurred. The transaction's process and user experience plays a key role in its success. If you can understand that concept, then you are well on your way to grasping the concept of identity and access management.

Oftentimes cybersecurity strategies focus on preventing access instead of ensuring those who should have access get it in a secure manner. As with gaining access to the airplane, the user experience, which involves the presentation and acceptance of the document, is a key component to any successful IAM strategy. Cybersecurity has been assigned a negative connotation of always telling the user no, but we have an opportunity with each IAM strategy to dispel that perception. The key to any successful IAM strategy in the borderless access age is to partner with a communications and change management team regardless of whether you are building an internal IAM or customer IAM (CIAM) strategy.

Leveraging communications and change management skill sets in developing and executing IAM strategies is based on a need to gain wide-scale adoption by the user population. Tools that should be included in these engagements include focus groups, user acceptance testing, and user surveys. Whether it be consumer or back office, today's user population usually consists of multiple generations that have different requirements for a successful user experience.

Today's digital landscape does not have any boundaries as it has permeated all areas of our lives. As if the lines weren't already blurred with so many connected devices, the coronavirus pandemic further increased the complexity with the significant expansion of remote work. From an IAM perspective, we have to change our mindset as identities have gone mobile and require access from multiple nontraditional locations and protection from various new threats on a daily basis. I recommend all cybersecurity professionals take a user experience course to better understand how to effectively address the user's needs in any IAM strategy. It can be the difference between failure and success.

Lessons from Cross-Training in Law

Danny Moules

After I began my journey in law six years ago, working as a freelance consultant at the time, I was struck looking back retroactively at legal advice I had given. Law is one of those topics, much like security itself, where a little knowledge can be a dangerous thing. It can be difficult to know where to draw the line as a professional who needs to provide advice promptly but also correctly.

Legal issues around InfoSec, such as privacy, crimes, forensics, etc., form an important part of many InfoSec roles. At a fundamental level, have you ever been asked if one is allowed to "hack [x]"? I have seen many respond quite confidently from various angles. Such a question seems innocuous enough, but there are underlying issues that the industry and lawmakers in every country are still grappling with.

Take a pen tester's perspective. Could you say, with legal certainty, a CFO (chief financial officer) is able to "authorize" the test? What if the scope included other parties? What happens if authorization is withdrawn during a test? I have seen many documents slapped together, often by people who couldn't answer these questions if challenged.

On September 11, 2019, a penetration testing team from Coalfire was asked to perform a penetration test of a Dallas County courthouse. In the course of their scoping discussion, physical infiltration of the building was believed, by the testers, to have been authorized. The State Court Administration "did not intend, or anticipate, those efforts to include the forced entry into a building" due to "different interpretations of the scope of the agreement."[1]

---

1 Charlie Osborne, "Pen Test Goes Pear-Shaped: Cybersecurity Firm Staff Arrested over Courthouse Burglary," September 16, 2019 (*https://oreil.ly/dV7XO*).

In response to an alarm, the testers were arrested breaking into a courthouse at midnight on September 11. They were charged with "burglary in the third degree and the possession of burglary tools." The charges were ultimately dropped, but it's a good example of the dangers of pushing up against the boundaries of legal precedent.

Were they allowed to "hack [x]"? It took a long court battle to answer that question.

Since I began studying law, my position on such topics has developed. I have insisted that scopes are signed off individually rather than by a general disclaimer. I have corrected clients trying to grant me permission to socially engineer third parties who could not legally have consented. I realized that many of my tools are subject to export restrictions and must be moved to hosts in the UK. I have familiarized myself with evidence law to ensure that my reports are "court ready" for my jurisdiction. These are just some examples.

Clearly I found I needed to know something of the law, but most InfoSec careers aren't going to leave time for law school, so what practical steps can be taken?

The most important advice I can offer is that instead of interpreting the law and synthesizing your own responses, you rely on trusted sources. The most reliable of these is, of course, lawyers, but I also recommend following legally responsible experts in your own specialist area. Consider brushing up on your understanding of common areas of law that come with your speciality, for the specific jurisdictions you work in. Certainly don't assume what you learn on a certification applies universally.

Second, consider that legal issues can be modeled and assessed like any other risk. Threat modeling your own services and procedures for legal problems isn't expensive and can help draw out legal risks.

Finally, make sure you know the limits of what advice you are allowed to give. In the UK, legal advice is not generally a protected activity, but this differs widely.

Ransomware

David McKenzie

Ransomware as a concept is very simple—a bully takes your stuff and you have to pay to get it back. In reality, it can quickly get complicated and murky. Pay or don't pay—should it be an ethical or business decision? Is it absolute or does it depend on circumstances?

History

Ransomware has been around since 1989. The first recorded attack, named the AIDS_Trojan or PC_Cyborg, was spread by floppy disks—the lure offered a risk analysis of an individual contracting AIDS, preying on the topical fear of developing the condition, by analyzing their lifestyle via a questionnaire. Once the system was infected, the virus waited until the machine had been rebooted 90 times before encrypting the local disk and triggering a pop-up that demanded $189 for the safe return of the files.

Ransomware became truly popular with the advent of cryptocurrency, when suddenly criminals didn't have to deal with account creation, money mules, or gift cards. Anybody could set up an "untraceable" cryptocurrency wallet and GET PAID. With early ransomware, the encryption methods were often written by the attacker and could at times be broken—some ransomware didn't encrypt at all, but simply changed the file extension. Over time, ransomware evolved, best practices such as "never roll your own crypto" came into play, and, today, reverse engineering often finds no solution to obtain the decryption key other than to pay the attacker.

Types of Ransomware

Fakes
> No files are encrypted—instead files are deleted as sabotage or as a cover for other malicious activities, often attributed to nation-state actors.

Encryptors
> Your data files are encrypted—you need to pay or restore from backups.

Blockers

Your entire system is encrypted and cannot be used at all as the operating system is locked out. This method is less popular since killing the victim's machine does make it harder to pay.

Stealers

Your files are encrypted (though some have now stopped bothering with this) and are also exfiltrated—you are threatened with public release if you do not pay.

Large-Scale Attacks

Company-wide attacks come from a breach, often phishing emails or unpatched perimeters. An attacker gains administrative privileges on the network and uses the network against itself, e.g., implementing group policy changes to disable the antivirus. A ransomware payload is sent to all machines, and data is exfiltrated. The ransomware is launched over a weekend or vacation. Threats appear and maybe a countdown timer urging "Pay or the files are leaked." Evidence that the attacker has the files, such as samples or screenshots, is presented via a ransom site.

Should You Pay?

In some cases, it will be illegal to pay. You will be criminally liable if you pay the ransom to certain "groups." It's been seen that "brokers" can sometimes be used to circumvent this, but should you really pay?

It's easy to say, "No, we don't negotiate with terrorists"—and that's what these actors are. Often this is organized crime, potentially linked with other serious activities—drugs and arms smuggling, people smuggling, and far worse. But what happens if you don't pay? The business goes under and thousands lose their jobs; the data of 100,000 people is leaked and they face becoming victims of identity theft, financial theft, or even bodily harm; or a hospital is left unable to perform lifesaving operations while in the throes of this attack. Pay and that hospital could be back up and running, saving lives, and their patients' confidential medical data will not be leaked.

The *right* answer is to say, "No, we will not pay."

Making that decision, and living with it, is sometimes harder.

The Key to Success in Your Cloud Journey Begins with the Shared Responsibility Model

Dominique West

Whether you are new to the cloud or a seasoned technology professional, fully understanding the shared responsibility model and how this framework plays a role in your organization's digital transformation is paramount. Rest assured you are not alone if hearing about this framework is new or understanding it has been confusing—many studies, including one by Help Net Security, have indicated that 7 out of 10 organizations have suffered a public cloud security incident in 2020 with 66% of them being the result of an exploited misconfiguration. So how can you make sure your organization is not part of this growing statistic? Let's take a look at what this framework is and how to put it into action.

What Is This Framework and Why Should It Apply?

Many organizations and security professionals have been following the perimeter-based model for quite some time (probably since the dawn of cybersecurity) and it makes sense as to why. Security largely has to do with control and pre-cloud era control involved everything inside of the organizational perimeter. Unfortunately, this model does not apply to our current digital age, as the cloud shatters your perimeter into a thousand pieces that can be difficult to keep up with. Alas, the shared responsibility model emerges as a way to help security professionals understand how security controls apply in the cloud.

The shared responsibility model is a framework that defines who is responsible for what when it comes to security in the cloud. Put simply, you, as the cloud user, and your cloud service provider (CSP), are accountable for different aspects of security for the cloud products you use. The level of accountability varies greatly depending on the service—for example, if you utilize a SaaS product you are typically only responsible for the data you use with this product, whereas the CSP is responsible for all other aspects of security across the tech stack needed to use the product. Conversely, if you use an Information as a Service (IaaS) product your level of security responsibility can increase exponentially and can cause potential data exposure if your responsibility is not fully understood. In fact, a study by KPMG found that only 8% of IT security leaders felt they fully understood the shared responsibility model. Not understanding cloud service functionality and placing your sensitive data in these products is one of the leading causes of misconfigurations and human errors. So to be on the safe side, make sure you know the different cloud computing service models and how security is managed in each.

How to Put This Framework into Action

Now that you know what the shared responsibility model is, and hopefully understand the different cloud service models as well, how can you put this framework into action as you accelerate your organization's journey to a cloud-first transformation? Begin by making sure you communicate your needs to your cloud service provider and understand the solutions being presented to solve them. Most cloud providers are transparent about their security responsibility with their products and if you are unsure, ask questions! Additionally, leverage tools as a way to mitigate human error in the cloud—both this framework and actual technologies that can manage, monitor, and alert for misconfigurations. Lastly, make sure your teams are getting the resources they need to be successful in this journey. Cloud digital transformations present a great opportunity to upskill your teams and get them engaged, so leverage them! Overall, beginning with this model will help you stay out of the headlines and keep your data secure.

Why InfoSec Practitioners Need to Know About Agile and DevOps

Fernando Ike

The release of the Agile Manifesto in 2001 was the consolidation of something that had already happened with many methods for application development such as extreme programming, Scrum, pragmatic programming, etc. They develop more efficient and robust features that the organization needs within a reasonable lead time. The Agile Manifesto was one of the foundation stones along with the internet revolution in the growth of digital-native organizations.

Over two decades after the Agile Manifesto, development and delivery features have become quicker than ever. This pressures operations IT teams to change their mindset and how they work, in order to know what developers and product managers were planning to deliver. Good communication and breaking silos have become essential skills.

In 2009, two events happened that changed how IT Operations must work:

- John Allspaw and Paul Hammond presented "10+ Deploys per Day: Dev and Ops Cooperation at Flickr" at the Velocity Conference.[1]
- Patrick Debois and others organized DevOpsDays in Ghent.[2]

Since then, we have seen new technologies, methods, and concepts concerning development, products, and operations. One key source organized by DORA Research and partners is the State of DevOps Report series.[3]

---

1 John Allspaw and Paul Hammond, "10+ Deploys per Day: Dev and Ops Cooperation at Flickr," Velocity, 2009 (*https://oreil.ly/8LIR4*).

2 DevOpsDays Ghent 2009 (*https://oreil.ly/OMwtJ*).

3 State of DevOps Reports (*https://oreil.ly/QjcDl*).

The 2019 DevOps State Report, organized by Google, shows us the four key metrics to software delivery performance and the values of elite performance organizations:

Metric	Value
Deployment frequency	On-demand (multiple deploys per day)
Lead time for changes	Less than one day
Time to restore service	Less than one hour
Change failure rate	0–15%

A big challenge for any organization is how to grow fast and improve software engineering. How can one execute that many deploys per day or recover quickly after a failure in one hour or less and execute security tasks? How do we implement tests within the pipeline with security tools like static application security testing (SAST), dynamic application security testing (DAST), Dependency-Check, etc., without increasing the lead time for commit? Adding more tests in the pipeline is an option that security people need to think about together with developers to find a good balance in the "Test Pyramid."[4]

People in security IT roles must involve the product or service phase and create a checklist for product teams to fill out. Now, more than ever, security IT professionals must participate in upstream sessions like Design Sprint or Lean Inception. These sessions are an opportunity for shared security concerns about products, services, and compliances; all in these sessions share responsibilities.

Soft skills are essential for security practitioners in high-performance organizations because they need to advocate for developers, sysadmins, testers, product managers, etc. Another important concept that needs to be advocated is the shared responsibility model that AWS establishes with its customers and users.[5] Security must be a concern for everyone in an organization.

Like ops teams that develop products or services as self-service platforms for developers to use, it will be more common for security teams to build platforms, so developers have a feedback loop about development time security issues.

---

4 Ham Vocke, "The Practical Test Pyramid," February 26, 2018 (*https://oreil.ly/nFKMH*).

5 "Shared Responsibility Model" (*https://oreil.ly/dAs65*).

Agile and DevOps are strongly influenced by Lean and the Toyota Production System. It's crucial for InfoSec people to learn how these concepts influence your discipline and the whole software engineering industry.

An example of how Lean influences the software engineering industry: pipelines (continuous delivery) are core to the value stream for elite organizations because it's their place to automate the process and inspect the build artifact for the next release. For instance, when you find anything that does not follow the quality expected or something that breaks a release in the pipeline, the pipeline is stopped and one checks what's broken and takes on tasks to fix the issue like the Andon Cord on the Toyota assembly line.

The Business Is Always Right

Frank McGovern

As a security professional, it is important to remember that the work you perform is for the business. This means that what you do almost always applies holistically to the organization. Businesses work in risk management while achieving their business objectives. Security falls into that vertical of risk management; it exists as an enabler for the business so that it can thrive by continuing at full speed in a world full of cybersecurity risks.

When we look at an organization, the leaders of them are essentially the business itself. A good chief executive officer views the company as their own. In some cases, such as private companies, this is exactly the case since they are typically the founders or owners of the business. When looking at a public company, it is often a board that has chosen who is best to be the head of the business. Leading involves determining what is the best direction and management of the organization. A responsibility of having this role is defining how risks are managed. This can be through several ways: accepting risk, transferring risk, mitigating risk, or avoiding risk.

While risk includes many things beyond security, your role in security is to help manage those risks associated to security. Even though many organizations are not managing security risk properly yet (e.g., not having a security risk register), the risks still exist and may be getting "cherry-picked" often from basic concepts or generalized industry guidelines.

All of this is meant to make you understand that even if you do not notice that you are doing risk management, you are. It may not be so obvious but choosing to implement an antivirus is you deciding that malware on machines is—or could be—a problem and then working to mitigate that risk. With that said, it is important to understand that risk management funnels up. What you consider a risk might not align with what your manager sees as a risk and the executive suite may also have a differing opinion.

There is much you can do to properly identify risks and speak to their actual quantification, that is, the actual likelihood and impact a risk can have to the business. This can be anything from simply putting a simple problem statement to a solution, building a formal security risk register, and/or even presenting risk management suggestions to one or many executives. In doing so, you might create a presentation or a well-written one-pager explaining the scenario and your business case. The executives' decision is to then decide what is best for the business. In some cases, the business (remember, leaders of a business are the business itself) may not agree with you. This could be for numerous reasons, even including the fact that you may not have properly reflected the risk and management option well enough. And that sucks. This is where it is important to remember that The Business Is Always Right, even if you think they are wrong or they actually are wrong and one day the risk hurts the business!

Take these opportunities where the business disagrees with you to perform a lessons learned. Only you and others who report to the executive(s) know them and what they like to see or hear. You can reflect on how you should better approach it next time. Even if you do not want to hear it, your role involves some sales skills sometimes. Most importantly, try not to take risk management personally by marrying yourself to your solutions. You can shed feelings by always remembering that "The business is always right."

Why Choose Linux as Your Secure Operating System?

Gleydson Mazioli da Silva

My first experience with Linux was in 1997 when I was looking for a more secure system to enter IRC channels on the internet without getting dropped by attacks. During my research, I found a hacking website where the author mentioned that he used Linux as his OS (operating system) and BitchX for IRC browsing. According to him, the system was like a battle tank.

I installed it and it was love at first sight. My PC became another one with the operating system. It stopped crashing or getting slow, and then I started replacing services that I professionally installed on Windows (Proxy, DNS, etc.) with equivalents using Linux.

I started to sleep better afterwards with the reduction of support tickets during nonwork hours. Linux, although new, was safe and reliable against attacks, so I decided to go deeper. Since its creation in 1991, Linus Torvalds has kept security as one the centerpieces of the operating system design, following the POSIX style (standard Unix variants).

Why is Linux the most secure? Let's go:

- Linux is the most chosen by cloud providers (which support thousands of virtual machines and containers), appliance manufacturers, and even NASA to equip a special bus and to build the reputation of your product and your business.

- There is total separation of privileges between programs that run on the system, and restriction of the use of resources (memory, processing, disk, network), avoiding exhaustion and unavailability caused by resource exhaustion or bugs in applications.

- Linux has access control lists (ACLs), attributes extended in filesystems, which allow advanced control of the permissions of what is written in the system, in addition to allowing the recording of metadata (hashes and other security parameters).

- Even if there are hardware failures (like Intel's recent ones), developers create mitigation methods within Linux to avoid exploiting some of them (as was the case with Specter).

- Linux uses an advanced mandatory security models (MAC) such as NSA SELinux, AppArmor, and Tomoyo. With these it is possible to control the use of resources by context, increasing the granularity of the security system to a level never seen in another OS.

- The use of well-configured security models makes Day 0 attacks unfeasible and reduces the risk of unscheduled stops or damage to the business.

- Security models use namespaces and cgroups for processes.

- Disk encryption use AES, which can be combined with Argon2. Your files will always be protected from prying eyes.

- Native support for any type of VPN is available on the market (from traditional IPsec to advanced OpenVPN and WireGuard).

- You can build resilience to various types of network attacks.

- You can protect against buffer overflows in memory using dynamic paging.

- Cgroups and namespaces are the basis for resource control in containerization. Without this, Docker, DevOps, and orchestration never would have existed.

- And a lot more! Not enough space to list all of them here!

Security professionals, SREs, pen testers, and DevSecOps use Linux as their primary system because basically they have everything they need at hand, and if it does not exist, it can quickly be written with the low-level access to the operating system.

I owe my career as an information security professional to the innovations brought by Linux, and new ones appear every day! And the best is that all this is at your fingertips for free, all well-documented and with a large community that can solve your doubts. Most of the devices in the world are somehow silently protected by a Linux system.

New World, New Rules, Same Principles

Guillaume Blaquiere

In the last decade, the world of information technology has pivoted from servers to virtualization to now cloud and serverless. However, most skilled security engineers understand that threats have been around even before servers were connected to the internet—remember when threats came by way of the floppy disk?

Bad actors and their teams are more organized, and the rapid evolution of tech has also created new attack possibilities. Threats have evolved.

With the introduction of the internet, the most significant threats no longer came from floppy disks but outside sources; this means that security teams have had to create and adapt their patterns continuously, for example, filtering and blocking external traffic with a firewall, sanitizing it, and then letting the traffic live in the internal DMZ (demilitarized zone).

Servers are now virtual machines, yet routers and firewalls are still the best defense methods for protecting IT resources. Virtualization in the cloud has not changed this; in fact, most if not all cloud providers propose IaaS (infrastructure as a service) with, at least, firewalls, routers, NAT, and VPNs. The old yet reliable DMZ pattern is still alive and well. The basics of IT security do not change as fast as the threats do—the tried and true formulas still work!

And then there was serverless.

Serverless, a disruptive proposition, basically tells us, "Hey, you don't have to manage virtual machines or the network; build your application and trust the cloud provider to handle the rest." What a Big Bang! This means:

- No network management
- No firewall rule to choose from
- No public IP access and limitation

- No addressing plan to discuss

- No DMZ

Twenty-year-old commonly accepted patterns, processes, and best practices are disappearing due to this new method of hosting applications. Suffice to say that security teams have had difficulties accepting this. Why? It's not because it's too new or because they have to trust a third party for their security management now, but because they have lost control of their domain. It's primarily a matter of understanding this new paradigm. Sure, the rules have changed, the frontiers of responsibilities have moved between the cloud providers and the companies, but the principles stay the same:

Don't expose the service publicly.
   This is no longer through public IP but with authorization filtering.

Don't expose your IP when performing external calls.
   NAT principles remain the same.

Keep your internal traffic safe.
   Internal no longer exists on managed infrastructure, so only accept connections from authenticated and authorized sources and services.

You can continue to enforce the old principles. They are all valid; only the implementations have evolved. Skilled security team members with years of experience and a core understanding of the basics are still very valuable, even in advisory matters. How else will we succeed in securing the new world?

The basics still matter.

Data Protection: Impact on Software Development

Guy Lépine

Stories of data breaches have plagued the news in recent years, up to a level that has made users lose faith in the security of applications and especially cloud applications. This is no surprise since data protection has had a lot of focus, thanks to the European General Data Protection Regulation, which mandates data processors to publicize the event, among other responsibilities. Therefore, data protection needs to remain a top priority to every software developer.

Secure Development

Fortunately, practices and tools are available to help release software applications with a high level of security. Microsoft introduced the *Security Development Lifecycle* about two decades ago, which has evolved ever since by adding practices at every phase of the life cycle, for example, gathering security requirements and modeling the threat during design in order to define additional acceptance criteria for the implementation phase. It has also evolved to define how to integrate into newer methodologies, such as Scrum Agile.

Cloud application developers should keep the periodically updated OWASP (Open Web Application Security Project) Top 10 close to them. The list describes the most probable risks associated with developing and operating a cloud application. For every risk, there are numerous references about detecting and preventing the risk occurrence.

Data Protection

Now that references to practices have been identified, let's focus on the lifetime of the data when processed by a software application.

There are three possible states:

1. At rest
2. In transit
3. In use

Data at rest

Data is put at rest using storage technology. They are numerous, but always end up saving the data on disk and providing abstraction features to manipulate it. For instance, when committing an SQL record update, a storage file will be updated and when creating a file in a *nix filesystem, a new inode is created to keep track of the data.

It is crucial for an application to identify the nature and location of the data when at rest, in order to use proper mitigation implementations. The nature of the data will dictate if specific processing requirements are needed, such as PC-DSS certification for credit cards or HIPAA privacy rules for patient records, while the location will, through the storage technology, define available mitigation technologies, such as filesystem access control systems or database field encryption functions.

Keep in mind that in this era of infrastructure as code, sensitive data may reside elsewhere within the application ecosystem. For instance, a stage may be required to provision service credentials within a container environment. It is obviously out of the question to commit these using the version control system containing the pipeline definition. A mitigation solution could be to leverage the dynamic injection available with a deployment toolset.

Data in transit

Data is in transit when it is transferred from an application's entity to another, usually using network protocols. These network protocols need to be carefully chosen and configured so information disclosure and tampering is improbable. For example, when exposing a REST API, the server side must be configured to listen on HTTPS. But only proper configuration of the protocol implementation will guarantee data security.

Data in use

Data is in use when a process is handling the data in memory. System designs must allow for process isolation and cross-process memory access. For instance, containerization isolates processes.

Ethical Data Access

Even though we put all the necessary controls in place, sensitive data will still need to be accessible by people, according to their roles in the team. We then need to make sure this data access is ethical. Audits need to be put in place in order to assess these accesses and make sure they remain appropriate.

An Introduction to Security in the Cloud

Gwyneth Peña-Siguenza

The building of the fundamental infrastructure for cloud services on a global scale has been one of the most significant architectural achievements in the past decade.[1] Its connections to the global internet rely on the capacity and security of all its networks, and it is essential that everyone assesses their cloud security in order to develop a strategy to protect their data.

Cloud security is a centralized security system that protects cloud-based systems against external and internal cybersecurity threats. It offers all of the functionality of traditional IT security, delivers 24/7 protection, and reduces administrative overhead.[2] Cloud security and security management best practices are designed to prevent unauthorized access to keep data private and safe across cloud-based infrastructure, applications, and platforms. The assessment of business resources and needs, through joint responsibility of the cloud customer and cloud solution provider, will determine the approach for integrating a comprehensive security strategy.

The full scope of cloud security, regardless of responsibility, is designed to protect the following components: physical networks, data storage, data servers, computer virtualization frameworks, operating systems, middleware, runtime environments, data, applications, and end-user hardware. These components are grouped into four main categories of cloud computing, with different levels of shared responsibility for security.

---

1 Tim Maurer and Garrett Hinck, "Cloud Security: A Primer for Policymakers," *Carnegie Endowment for International Peace*, 29-38, August 2020 (*https://oreil.ly/RqCVh*).

2 "What Is Cloud Security?," *Forcepoint* (*https://oreil.ly/9l4EF*).

These include:

- Public cloud services (operated by a public cloud provider)[3]
  - Software as a service (SaaS): it is the customer's responsibility to secure their data and user access.
  - Infrastructure as a service (IaaS): it is the customer's responsibility to secure their data, user access, applications, operating systems, and virtual network traffic.
  - Platform as a service (PaaS): it is the customer's responsibility to secure their data, user access, and applications.
- Private cloud services (operated by a third party)
- Private cloud services (operated by internal staff)
- Hybrid cloud services (operated by internal staff and optional public cloud solution provider)

Cloud customers may choose a model based on their particular needs and will find that different types of data require different levels of security.

The emergence of various new tools allows attackers to detect and target vulnerabilities in the cloud. Challenges that arise in maintaining a secure cloud include:[4]

- There is full visibility into the cloud service or cloud data.
- In a third-party cloud solution provider environment, there is limited control by cloud customers by default and no access to the underlying physical infrastructure.
- User access can be from any location or device; this privileged access by cloud provider personnel could bypass internal security controls.
- The cloud environment must adhere to regulatory requirements and internal compliance as well as risk management processes.
- The exploitation of errors or vulnerabilities in the cloud deployment without the use of malware can enable attackers access through weakly configured or protected interfaces.

---

3 "What Is Cloud Security?," McAfee (*https://oreil.ly/PD7s2*).

4 Ibid.

- There are misconfigurations such as lack of access restrictions, vulnerable APIs due to inadequate or insufficient authorization, data loss, or poor access management.

Cloud security is networked, concentrated, and shared and the responsibility for risk in the cloud is shared between customers and cloud solution providers.[5] Security issues in the cloud cover a spectrum ranging from failure and unavailability to limited performance or effects limited to subsets of data and services. Consequences vary vastly across incidents depending on which customers and which data or services are affected. It is essential that organizations have full confidence in their cloud computing security, and that all data, systems, and applications are protected from data theft, leakage, corruption, and deletion.[6]

The widespread adoption of cloud computing transformed both companies and hackers, bringing a gamut of opportunities as well as security risks.[7] Through comprehensive security policies, solutions, and an organizational culture of security, companies can leverage the benefits of cloud computing necessary to stimulate innovation and collaboration.

---

5 Maurer and Hinck, "Cloud Security: A Primer for Policymakers."

6 "What Is Cloud Security?," *Forcepoint.*

7 Cypress Data Defense, "7 Cloud Computing Security Vulnerabilities and What to Do About Them," *Towards Data Science*, July 13, 2020 (*https://oreil.ly/SWknr*).

Knowing Normal

Gyle dela Cruz

If you work in the blue team or cyber defense side of information security, you will inevitably be involved in doing some investigations. It could involve network intrusion or malware infections. No matter what type of investigations you do, an understanding of what is normal will form a significant aspect of your work. Protecting the triad of confidentiality, integrity, and availability forms the basic tenets of InfoSec. Keeping the information confidential, accurate, and available is the norm we aspire to.

You will need to know what normal looks like when it comes to network protocols, computer operations, application behavior, and even the traffic flow in your corporate environment. An attack will affect what is normal. Think of the attack as the anomaly in your setup. All detection tools rely on having specifications on what is considered unusual or not normal. Think of the signatures or rules from your IPS (intrusion prevention system) and anti-malware platforms that will alert upon a match on malicious activity.

Having a set of baseline information helps us understand what is normal. For example, there are standards written for the implementation of a network protocol. Common attack tools will subvert the standards. Having the capability to look at a packet capture and understand the flow of traffic will lead you to find indicators of malicious network traffic. If you need to analyze a Windows host for malware infection, the knowledge of what the common parent-child processes are will help you figure out what is a legitimate process, and what is suspicious and must be further investigated. Knowing the traffic trends in your environment will help you understand whether the unusual volume of traffic going out is part of a backup across your WAN connections or something else.

How do we gather all this information? Document what is in your corporate environment: applications, software, network diagrams. Then get approval to run some packet-sniffing tools or use NetFlow information from your network devices to gather the baseline for your network. Use Wireshark and read the RFCs or other documentation for the protocols to help you in dissecting the packets. Find out what the typical software or applications installed on the desktops and servers are. Use free tools like Process Monitor or Redline to capture the process details while you are simulating a typical end-user activity. Then analyze the data to know what processes start when certain applications are used. Take time to understand what the daily tasks of employees in different departments are and what patterns they leave behind in the system or network. This will make it easier to catch insider threats when employees who should not access certain resources suddenly start connecting to the supposedly off-limits data.

All of the data that you collected serves as a guideline on what is normal in your environment. This along with all the reading and experimentation you've done will help you know what is normal. One last thing: remember to figure out how your tools work so that if you suspect that the telemetry is a bit off, you can fine-tune the rules or fix your tool.

All Signs Point to a Schism in Cybersecurity

Ian Barwise

A schism is a division or disunion, especially into mutually opposed parties.

The cybersecurity industry is at a crossroads. Each week there are new reports of data breaches and ransomware attacks that expose personally identifiable information (PII) and personal health information (PHI) as well as financial, proprietary, password, and sensitive information that is very damaging to individuals, organizations, and governments across all industries. We will continue to see the effects of these breaches for years to come.

But it's not as if computers or networks and the technical protocols they operate on are new inventions and it's not as though cybersecurity is some new field of study. Information and communications technology (ICT) has been around for decades and the entire time it has existed, there have been vulnerabilities that have been consistently exploited by criminal hackers. It's not new; this is an old game of whack-a-mole. You patch one hole and hackers pop up through another.

There is a schism that has formed within the information security industry and the rest of the world, including commercial industry, government, and criminal enterprises. As employers' performance expectations continue to rise and they continue to complain about a self-perceived "skills gap" there is a mountain of evidence to support the fact that employers don't understand cybersecurity, don't write their job requirements correctly, and aren't willing to pay cybersecurity professionals competitive salaries or offer them quality benefits. Meanwhile, cyber threat actors could care less about any of this. They see your organization's lack of a coherent, well-defended network as a juicy target that is ripe for exploitation.

Attackers Have Always Had the Advantage

Sourcegraph surveyed 500 North American software developers and revealed that software devs in 2020 are now managing 100 times more code than they did in 2010.[1] That is just insane to think about. Imagine if you had to penetration test 100 times more systems a year just to earn the same amount of salary you make now. How about if you had to manage and monitor 100 times more information systems?

It's daunting to think about, yet everyone is quick to point fingers at the devs who write the code that gets exploited. Mind you, salaries have not gone up 100 times since 2010, but employers expect employees to perform much more each year. Sound fair to you? When people ask why there seems to be a never-ending amount of exploitable vulnerabilities in software applications, it's not difficult to understand why.

Humans are fallible and can't possibly be expected to write that much code quickly and proofread it for accuracy as they go. We are not machines. "But there are tools for checking code," you say. Yes, of course. We are aware. Like artificial intelligence and machine learning, however, these tools and capabilities are only as good as the code and biased algorithms we program them to operate with.

The pressure on devs to produce, produce, produce is unreal. The tempo of DevSecOps in some of the organizations I've worked in is unreal, even unsustainable I would venture to say. Burnout is coming for you! "Just get the code to production, we can patch the flaws later!" I can hear the Scrum Masters now. Another team will take care of fixing your code flaws. There is room in the Agile software development process for security to be overlooked. Continuous improvement of the tools that we use to check code is imperative as well.

---

1 Jim Salter, "Sourcegraph: Devs Are Managing 100x More Code Now Than They Did in 2010," *Ars Technica*, October 1, 2020 (*https://oreil.ly/tKfxf*).

DevSecOps Is Evolving to Drive a Risk-Based Digital Transformation

Idan Plotnik

Digital transformation has become a board-level discussion. Executives realize that their businesses are being disrupted, and they need to innovate faster than ever in order to gain a competitive advantage and drive consistent growth. DevOps has become synonymous with delivering faster in an Agile manner, but a secure software development life cycle (SDLC) has often been left behind in the constant struggle for speed because it contains manual processes and too many tools that lack the context of risk and business impact. In addition, they are handled by different practitioners in the organization (e.g., developers, security architects, and compliance officers).

DevSecOps is the methodology and practice of inserting security into the DevOps process. Many organizations have found some level of success by automating their existing security processes and calling it "DevSecOps," but that approach has created other issues, including more alerts and false positives that the security and development teams don't have the time to research and fully understand in order to effectively remediate risk. With a ratio of one security architect for every 100 developers, DevSecOps has struggled to effectively scale.

Code Security Is Becoming "Security"

What modern DevSecOps practitioners understand is that now everything is code! Product managers and developers are no longer writing detailed design documents. The code is the design. Infrastructure is now code. Cloud security settings are now defined in code. Adding personally identifiable information (PII) to a data model, publishing a new API in a cloud API gateway, and configuring authorization controls are all now done in code. This is what is finally enabling DevSecOps to live up to its initial promise. Code can be scanned. Rules can be established and processes automated. Machine learning (ML) and natural language processing (NLP) can be applied to detect abnormalities and risky material changes. Workflows can ensure that the right people are focused on the right security issues.

Shifting from Vulnerabilities to Risky Code Changes

In its early stages, DevSecOps was focused on finding *vulnerabilities* but state-of-the-art practitioners are moving past that to focus on risky changes and their business impact. Static and dynamic code analysis, fuzzing, and software composition analysis tools have focused on vulnerabilities and are now only part of a broader analysis of real-world risk. Context matters. And as development gets even faster, it matters more and more. This is a significant shift.

Code Risk Is Multidimensional

Properly evaluating code risk requires more than surface scans. It involves a deep understanding of the code components, security controls, data, and developer expertise. But in addition to focusing on code, security architects and AppSec engineers are broadening their roles to encompass all data that can help drive better decision making. "Shifting left" requires analyzing data from the design all the way through the SDLC phases to production, including container security, cloud configurations, API gateway settings, and more. Other security domains are bringing their unique capabilities into DevSecOps. User and entity behavior analytics (UEBA) concepts are being used to identify compromised developer accounts and insider threats. Reverse engineering is being used to identify code that was inserted during the continuous integration and continuous delivery (CI/CD) pipeline. NLP is used to evaluate risk in Jira tickets, commit messages, and pull requests.

DevSecOps Is Evolving

Like many new methodologies, DevSecOps has made its way through cycles of hype and disillusionment but has evolved to become an essential tool that brings together development, security, and compliance teams to meet risk management requirements while enabling teams to accelerate business transformation.

Availability Is a Security Concern Too

Jam Leomi

One thing I remind people of when looking at the three pillars of security, consisting of confidentiality, availability, and integrity (CIA): the one that holds the other two up is *availability*. As our industry continues its time of cloud-based infrastructure, applications, and SaaS-y services, security should keep in mind that uptime also equals things staying available and online, not just operations. It ensures that everybody at the company gets paid and that the business grows. So, as a security practitioner who should be holistically thinking about operations when architecting a program, one must consider all the different ways availability can be impacted in this current (and future) world we live in.

The first issue is ensuring that any security operational changes we make don't impact the company. That's ensured by, of course, collaborating with teams to ensure that changes made don't have adverse impacts. At one place I worked, even after testing, rolling out firewall changes company-wide resulted in a hard downtime because none of the Ops team knew of the rollout, which resulted in a longer investigation and uncovering unknowns. While it was a learning experience, it definitely could have helped to give the team a forewarning that availability could be impacted or that the change should be monitored.

The second issue is ability to support and have services available to the company, come what may. In the time right now where a good portion of the US and other countries are working at home due to the pandemic, it's becoming even more important to think about how to keep security operations running. Though zero-trust technologies exist, how are you communicating those mechanisms to the team and ensuring trust of those systems? How are we training people to understand alternatives in case some services go wrong or go down? How are we ensuring that reporting can still happen even if a user who's investigating is remote with an unreliable connection? We have to consider the variables in availability here when providing those services to the company and our team.

And finally, availability includes our own well-being. As security folk, we tend to always be on high alert, so taking care of our mental and physical wellbeing is important. I myself have been through the thing of working myself into the ground, being on high alert with some device always nearby, just in case. Speaking from personal experience, it only leads to a phone you constantly keep on silent. It isn't healthy to constantly be that way, though there are moments it's required. So, just as we plan recovering availability from an incident or change, we should also do that for ourselves. I don't know what that looks like for every individual, especially not being a medical professional, but this would be a good time to reach out to one (or a few) you trust.

So, now with all those things discussed, go forth! And remember: availability is a security problem that impacts in multiple ways; but you can be prepared if you work with folks as well as with yourself.

Security Is People

James Bore

The biggest thing that people forget about security is that on a very fundamental level *it* is about people.

You will sometimes hear statements like "people are the weakest link," or "your strongest defense," or a myriad of other sayings. What all of these tend to overlook is that, if we consider security as the art and science of protecting an asset from a threat, ultimately the only threat out there is more people (excluding aliens), and the only assets we are looking to protect are yet more people.

You'll hear people, processes, and technology bandied around a lot, and it's important to view people as the most important of those three. If your processes hinder the people who belong in your asset group, then your assets will find workarounds and become threats. If your processes aid those in your threats group, then you are helping them to target your assets.

Everything that you do in security you should be able to associate directly to one of two goals:

- Empowering your asset people to achieve their aims
- Disempowering your threat people

When you start to look at security through this lens, the people-focused lens, things change. Constraints that are placed because they are considered best practice often become unnecessary, while things that might be overlooked (updating your password policy to passphrases with a good communications rollout plan) become priorities.

When working with the rest of the organization, this lens makes a huge difference. Remember, the organization does not exist to enact security; security exists to help secure the aims of the organization, which are realized through the people who make it up. When security becomes an obstacle to people in the organization, it becomes an obstacle *for* the organization, and people work around it. When, instead, it becomes a sensible precaution and set of practices that people understand the reasons for and how it protects them, the value becomes obvious.

When the value of security is being questioned within an organization, a solution is never to double down on enforcement. Bringing in additional constraints and obstacles increases the resentment, with good reason. The focus must be on educating people on why security matters to them, personally. Stamping people into shape does not lead to them following good practices, nor doing their best towards common goals.

If you run into the occasional problem where someone will fundamentally not accept following security practices, there are really two options. Either that person should not be within the organization, or the practice needs to be reconsidered. Sometimes there are just people unwilling to act in their own best interests, whether that's because you are unable to convince them, or simply because their personal risk appetite is at odds with the risk appetite of the organization.

The big takeaway here is simple. If you come across some practice in security and cannot point to how it protects your asset people from your threat people enough to justify any obstacles it puts in the way of your assets, think very carefully about whether it is necessary in the first place.

Penetration Testing: Why Can't It Be Like the Movies?!

Jasmine M. Jackson

What is the first thought when hearing the words "penetration testing"?

Penetration testing in the general sense exploits vulnerabilities that are found in computer systems. A vulnerability is a flaw in a computer system. An analogy to a vulnerability is if you're not at home but you leave your window open. It's a vulnerability as one can go through your window and enter your home. In our analogy, a penetration test would be a burglar entering your home through the open window to steal items from your home.

When most people hear penetration testing their minds automatically go to television shows or movies they have watched where the character opens a command prompt and starts typing commands. The character automatically finds the perfect exploit to gain access to the system. After gaining access to the system, they're able to find the pertinent information and everything is well. Is this how it works in the real world? No. In reality, there are five phases of penetration testing—information gathering, reconnaissance, discovery and scanning, exploitation, and reporting.

From the five phases, the most important is reconnaissance. The reason for this is you need to know your target before exploiting it. I made this mistake early on when learning penetration testing, by skipping the first three phases and starting at the fourth—exploitation. Doing this, I spent many nights banging my head on the wall.

The important thing I learned with penetration testing is to have a series of steps or methodology. But here's a caveat—don't get so fixated on the methodology that you develop tunnel vision. An example of this is that the obvious and easiest answer might be the best approach to gain entry into a computer system.

When I first started to learn how to conduct penetration tests, I fell into the trap of having tunnel vision. I always wanted to use the most elegant exploits after completing the scanning and discovery phase. I would spend hours googling and crafting the exploit only to find that the obvious answer would allow me to gain entry to the system in less than 5 minutes.

So we've found the exploit and are in the system and able to do damage. We're done, right? Wrong. The final phase of penetration testing is to complete the report. The report will have an executive summary of the penetration testing engagement, along with the vulnerabilities found inside the computer system. These vulnerabilities will be ranked by severity (high, medium, and low) with reproduction steps on how the vulnerability was exploited.

When I write my reports, I write them for the absolute beginner. My rule of thumb is the reproduction steps should allow the reader to go from A to Z and understand in a general sense what is going on. I see a lot of times where the reproduction steps are not clearly defined or assumptions are made about the audience of the report. It's important to write the report as general as possible as the entire organization will read the report from the CISO to the developer.

There's a lot more to penetration testing than just exploiting the system. You will need to do research on your target. Find the exploit, and actually exploit the system. Finally, you will need to create a report to share how vulnerable the system is so organizations can prioritize how they want to remediate their system. Too bad penetration testing is not as easy as it's displayed on television and the movies where the computer system is readily available to be exploited.

How Many Ingredients Does It Take to Make an Information Security Professional?

Jasmine M. Jackson

What makes a good security professional? Some would say to have security certifications as long as your name. Others would say that you have to be born with it. Neither of these statements are true. There are information security professionals who are high school drop-outs, high school graduates, and college graduates. What do all of these groups have in common? They have specific ingredients to make them great information security professionals. Want to know the ingredients? Well keep reading.

The first ingredient is to have a *thirst for knowledge*. Many information security professionals take on the quest of learning a subject to become a master in it. This drive or quest will never go away. As their understanding of the subject grows, so does their depth of knowledge.

The second ingredient is *finding a niche* in information security. The information security field is very broad and vast. Sample subject areas are application security, forensics, and risk and governance. Good information security professionals master one subject and have a breadth of knowledge in other subject areas. This extensive knowledge will allow the information security professional to not be siloed or close-minded in their approach to solving problems.

The third ingredient is *passion*. There will be days where it seems you're not making any progress and in some instances feel like you're going backwards. There will be other times where the subject matter will completely frustrate you to where you will abandon your efforts. When this happens, passion will be the ingredient to draw motivation to continue learning and moving forward.

The fourth ingredient is *take risks within reason*. There's a quote, "Nothing grows in the comfort zone." It's true. While the comfort zone gives the perception of warm and fuzzies like a nice hot blanket, in reality it's an anchor around one's neck that binds you to familiarity and possibly outdated thinking. It's OK to take risks, as it should be a bit scary/intimidating at first glance. Taking risks is one of the best ways to grow in your career and as a person.

The fifth and final ingredient is *learning how to fail fast*. In a perfect world, everything works right the first time. Unfortunately, we do not live in a perfect world and can only make decisions on our knowledge at the time. Due to blind spots, there will be problems we try to solve where we don't know all of the information and have to make educated guesses. Sometimes those guesses work but there will be other times where the guesses are totally off. When this happens, an information security professional will need to assess why the situation failed and learn from it. Information security is a cyclic process where we acquire knowledge and make adjustments as we see fit. Good information security professionals do not dwell in their mistakes; rather they get invigorated to get it right the next time.

Having the above five ingredients is a start in having a good career in information security. By no means is this list exhaustive. This article shows anyone with a desire to learn about information security can be successful in this field. The professional needs to find an area of information security that interests them and learn as much information as they can.

Understanding Open Source Licensing and Security

Jeff Luszcz

The explosion of open source software has changed every company into a software company.

The impact of this change in how software is procured has caused many organizations to struggle with managing the sheer quantities of components and packages that they now depend on.

As an information security professional, it is important to understand the impacts on security that open source may have as it is selected, downloaded, and updated while at the same time being aware of legal or business risks that may also be introduced into the company.

Software packages and libraries are controlled by licenses. These licenses may be commercial or open source (OSS). Open source (or quasi-open source) licenses typically fall into three styles:

- Permissive (allows use with few obligations, often simply just passing along a copyright notice)
- Copyleft/viral (requires source code to be shared with users and the community if the code is used)
- Restrictive (restricts certain actions or use cases)

The last style is not technically open source but is often mixed in and confused as an open source project.

The heart of a successful OSS management program is keeping a current and continuous inventory of OSS packages. This inventory, often called the software bill of materials (SBOM), allows you to keep on top of software updates and vulnerabilities, reducing security risk. It also allows you to manage license policy, reducing legal and business risk.

OSS may be brought in by your company's developers, through third-party applications or external vendors. All of these require management either by your own team, or by requiring bills of materials from your third-party vendors.

Some security-related static or dynamic application security testing (SAST/DAST) tools can provide a limited open source bill of materials. While these reports are often limited in scope, they can provide a good on-ramp to managing your open source dependencies. Many companies use software composition analysis (SCA) tools to explicitly discover and manage their open source dependencies.

Both commercial and OSS scanning tools exist and should be part of your security strategy. Companies are often shocked by the number of dependencies that are discovered, so time should be budgeted for managing the alerts that are emitted by the scanners. You should plan on discovering dozens to hundreds of previously unknown dependencies when you first examine a system. There is often an initial wave of fixes required, and then a continuous periodic slow drip of new alerts as OSS components "age out" and require security updates.

It is important to confirm that a new version of a component is compatible with the rest of the stack your system depends on, and that its license has not changed to one that is restricted in your organization.

Your organization should have an Open Source License policy that will inform you of the licenses that are allowed or restricted. A license's terms and your license policy often depends on your use case and distribution model.

New standards for the maintenance of open source dependencies such as the OpenChain Project (*https://oreil.ly/zM7J4*) are making the process of OSS compliance easier and more unified.

By understanding how open source is licensed, maintained, and updated you can minimize risks to your organization while at the same time allowing for the use of open source. As an information security professional, you will often find yourself needing to weigh in on the security impacts caused by outside vulnerabilities. By understanding OSS licensing and security, you are in a better position to make correct decisions when these events arise.

Planning for Incident Response Customer Notifications

JR Aquino

Incident response is a discipline around managing a crisis. The core of this activity is to provide a central control point for information and alignment on execution using the best information available at the time. We should first start by disambiguating an internal incident versus a customer or third-party impacting incident, which requires notifications to those affected.

When harm has befallen your company's data, infrastructure, or service(s) and there is *no impact to third parties*, upon remediation, the event could be considered contained and may only require internal recordkeeping for compliance purposes.

When harm has befallen your customer's service, data, or personally identifiable data your company manages, you may have an obligation to report the incident to the impacted third parties and/or regulators. These are the cases that are most sensitive and require coordination to ensure that contractual, regulatory, and business obligations are all fulfilled.

It's useful to note here that most incidents you encounter will have no "hacker" involved. Most of the incidents that you are likely to manage will be due to human error.

Let's dive right in and establish the core fundamentals that you will need to prepare for a security incident that requires notifications.

Assume breach.

The first order of business is to "assume breach." What I mean here is to have a plan of action with necessary steps so that in the event of a crisis, you already have the documentation and training prepared ahead of time:

- Have an incident response plan documented.
- Create a status update template.
- Keep a contact list with a roles and responsibilities matrix up to date.

Keep the business up to date.
There are going to be a lot of different activities going on during a crisis. Keeping track of all these workstreams and articulating them to leadership is paramount.

- Make sure compliance staff is aware and tracking audit evidence.
- Ensure your legal representation is engaged.
- Establish expectations of a rhythm of status updates (e.g., hourly, daily, weekly, etc.).

Identify the impacted parties.
- Enumerate how many entities are affected.
- Differentiate between first and third parties.
- Attribute contact info to the impacted data assets.

Prepare your staff for external parties reaching out about the incident
Once communications have gone out, there will be an influx of inbound support requests from those who were notified.

- Establish talking points for customer-facing staff like support and sales.
- If you have a PR or comms team, make sure they're engaged.
- Monitor social media and news outlets.

Keep a detailed timeline of events.
- When does the evidence indicate the event occurred?
- When did the company become aware of the event?
- When were steps taken to contain, mitigate, and remediate the incident?

Publish customer communications.
- Work with the stakeholders to ensure you have an accurate depiction of the impact, the affected parties, and the steps that have been taken and/or planned.
- Stakeholders should be contributing to the comms: engineering/legal/comms/security/compliance/business leadership.

Perform a post-incident review (PIR): improvement goals.

It may not feel like it at the time, but every incident is a gift. Each incident you face gives you an opportunity to improve your processes. Perform a post-incident review to continuously improve your program.

- Identify steps that could eliminate or reduce the risk of the incident reoccurring.
- Identify improvements needed to diagnose the incident, including service impacted, priority level, and the correct resolver teams to be engaged.
- Ensure incident communication was proper or if anything can be improved.
- Update the incident response standard operating procedures (SOP).

Managing Security Alert Fatigue

Julie Agnes Sparks

A Security Incident Response Team (SIRT) can be one of the greatest assets of a company, but it is also a *finite* resource. Each security engineer or analyst can only investigate a set number of alerts. Whenever these alerts stretch beyond what is feasible to investigate or the alerts are never indicators of actual security incidents, your team will become overwhelmed with alert fatigue. Alert fatigue can cause exhaustion, general demotivation, and lower quality investigations.

Often a security operations team's success is measured by how many threat intelligence feeds they ingest, how many detections they write, and how many alerts they create. But why alert on every "bad" domain no matter how stale when you have folks who can write detections on malicious patterns specific to your environment? When the value of a security team is based on the volume, rather than the quality, of what they produce, that team is effectively set up for failure. Managers should instead design goals and metrics that encourage high-quality detections, and push back on requests that will increase noise such as ingesting everything into a security incident and event management (SIEM) tool. High-noise detections generate many false positives, which throttles the amount of bandwidth a security team has to investigate real incidents and improve processes. By measuring teams on the amount of input, the quality of the output diminishes and alert fatigue increases. While every organization is different and there is no universal standard, I've found that low to medium noise detections generally produce less than five alerts a day. The amount of alerts will increase based on the size of your organization; however, if a detection is producing dozens of alerts an hour, it falls into the "high noise" category and is most likely an ineffective indicator of a security incident.

What are the best ways to avoid alert fatigue?

- Deploy security detections that have low levels of noise. If they are noisy, continue to refine and reduce scope until the detections are more meaningful.
- Prioritize security alerts that are more likely to indicate a real attack.
- Enrich alerts with as much information as possible to make it easier to determine whether the activity is malicious.
- Build automations that remove as many steps for the security analysts as possible.
- Leverage your employees to confirm their own behavior through automation where appropriate.
- When automation isn't feasible, create and diligently maintain playbooks for how employees are expected to investigate security alerts.
- Have a contingency plan for how to reallocate resources in various scenarios, such as when there is an active security incident but there are still alerts coming in that need to be monitored.
- Adopt the follow the sun (FTS) model. Don't have North American–based employees answering alerts and responding to incidents for countries in Asia.

By minimizing the amount of alert fatigue, you will set up your security engineers for success, provide meaningful work, and have a more robust approach to handling security alerts and investigations.

Take Advantage of NIST's Resources

Karen Scarfone

NIST, the National Institute of Standards and Technology, is a US government agency working in many areas of science, technology, and measurement. It has been conducting security research and releasing publicly available, copyright-free security guidance and other resources since the early 1970s. Today NIST is known all over the world for its security expertise.

No matter your level of knowledge—from a security newbie to a guru—I guarantee NIST has resources for you that you've never seen before. The NIST Computer Security Resource Center (CSRC) (*https://oreil.ly/pDiQZ*), is the home for most of the resources. As of this writing, they include 84 project sites and 677 security publications on just about every security topic imaginable, from hardware roots of trust to the security of IoT consumer devices, and from work-from-anywhere security to the development of quantum-resistant cryptographic algorithms. CSRC also contains archived publications going all the way back to NIST's earliest security work. If you use the CSRC search interface, you can choose to see "Withdrawn" publications, and at present there are 654 of them. Some of these publications provide a fascinating view into how security has changed over the past 50 years.

Need to know what a security-related term or acronym means? No problem! CSRC offers an online glossary with definitions of nearly 8,000 terms and acronyms, and it cites the source of each definition so you can learn more about the topic if you're interested. CSRC is also the home for NIST frameworks like the Risk Management Framework (RMF), the Cybersecurity Framework (CSF), and the Privacy Framework. Each of these frameworks has been widely adopted by government, industry, and other organizations around the world, and CSRC offers not only documents that define the frameworks, but also implementation guides, training materials, webinars, and case studies.

Another resource that NIST offers is the National Vulnerability Database (NVD) (*https://nvd.nist.gov*). NVD provides information on over 100,000 publicly disclosed software vulnerabilities. NVD analysts rate each vulnerability's relative severity using the Common Vulnerability Scoring System (CVSS) to help organizations prioritize vulnerability mitigation. The NVD data is also widely used by researchers to analyze trends in vulnerability characteristics.

In addition to all of those NIST resources—and many more there isn't room to even mention here—NIST also has the National Cybersecurity Center of Excellence (NCCoE). NCCoE focuses on finding practical technology solutions to real-world security problems. A typical NCCoE project brings together representatives from industry, academia, government, and others to design, implement, and test proof-of-concept solutions in lab environments. Then the collaborators publish detailed information on the proof-of-concepts to *https://nccoe.nist.gov*. Many NCCoE projects are sector-specific, like securing industrial IoT for the energy sector or securing remote patient monitoring for the healthcare sector. Other projects are cross-cutting, such as supply chain assurance, 5G security, and zero trust architecture.

Take an hour to wander through NIST's resources and see what catches your attention. There's always more to learn and constantly new resources being released. NIST also offers numerous mailing lists you can join to keep up with the latest in CSRC and NCCoE updates, not to mention all the workshops, industry days, webinars, and other events that NIST hosts.

Apply Agile SDLC Methodology to Your Career

Keirsten Brager

Back in the day, employees could plan to work for one or two companies over their entire careers. The paths were linear and typically well-defined, providing a clear path to achieve performance-based or tenure-related promotions. Those days are over, so you must plan accordingly.

Instead of expecting your career to follow a linear or a sequential path, I propose we start normalizing the application of the Agile methodology to our careers. Using this framework, careers are planned in two- to four-year sprints with clearly defined goals and iterations along the way. Flexibility is built into the design, and the small sprints include a focus on gaining specific skill sets, networking opportunities, and closing the pay equity gap. There are plenty of studies and social media conversations to illustrate how staying at one company stunts income growth. If companies will not pay and promote equitably, then employees should be comfortable applying the Agile SDLC methodology to promote themselves regularly.

Secure Your Identity and Assets

New people and those interested in the field: one of the best ways to learn about securing endpoints and identities is to start by protecting your own:

- Secure your home network.
- Disable unnecessary ports and services.
- Harden your personal devices: most product have online guides.
- Review and update privacy settings on accounts and devices.
- Use multifactor authentication where possible.

Learning by doing will keep your family safe and prepare you for the certifications and interviews you are going to have. It will also give you topics to publish content about, which could help attract the opportunities you're trying to secure.

Look for Unconventional Paths

Most people decide to set their targets on employment at the biggest and most popular companies. If you are just starting out, why choose the path of most resistance?

Meanwhile, your local utility companies need people to help them protect essential services: electricity, water, and gas. Governments at the federal, state, and local levels are also hiring.

While these entities may not offer the high salaries or popularity of the largest tech companies, they do important work that we all depend on for our very survival.

Utilities and governments also do business with many of the large tech companies, so those internal relationships could also be leveraged to gain access to the next phase of your career sprint.

Although the "shortage of talent" conversation has become clickbait at this point, there is absolutely a shortage of industrial control systems/operational technology (ICS/OT) security talent. Many utility and manufacturing companies are just starting to establish OT security teams and dedicating the required funding. If you've never considered this path before, now is a good time to start looking beyond the limited number of popular security teams on your social media feeds.

Career transition folks—stop underestimating your value:

- Your sales experience is transferable to product-specific roles.
- Your customer service experience translates well in governance, risk, and compliance (GRC) jobs.
- Your administrative skills are great for IT project management.
- Your analytical and writing skills are great for policy analyst roles.

Do not make your career more difficult than it must be following the crowd. Chart your own unconventional path and reap the rewards of the seeds you planted.

Failing Spectacularly

Kelly Shortridge

We all would love to eradicate failure in our systems, but it is impossible. We will never eliminate all vulnerabilities in software, remove the potential for abuse in all intended functionality, nor ensure humans do not make mistakes that jeopardize security in the course of their work. Any security program built on those quixotic assumptions will inevitably fail. Instead, we must prioritize our capacity to be resilient to failure.

When the mission is to stop any failure from happening, there is no room for innovation. This mission is why we see too many security practitioners pretending that revenue, profit, and other business concerns are irrelevant to their work. When security views itself as a separate, noble entity from the rest of the business, colleagues are transformed from potential collaborators into potential bad apples or rivals. It means that security strategies, tools, architectures, and policies ignore business concerns, resulting in the self-fulfilling prophecy of other teams "not caring" about this intrusive, inefficient security.

Security practitioners are not exempt from propelling business success. A successful long-term business is one that can weather failure gracefully and come out stronger for it. A business that avoids failure at all costs inevitably stagnates, as there is no room for risk to pursue growth and innovation.

Security Chaos Engineering represents a critical shift in how we think about digital defense. Failure is a learning opportunity full of invaluable insight that can help us refine and reinforce our systems. Proactively introducing failure into systems through chaos experiments fuels that feedback loop. It builds muscle memory among our teams for responding to security incidents, thereby reducing stress and burnout. It transforms the shadowy monster of the unknown into a workable problem with established solutions that become routine after repeated practice.

Information security work is often analogized to a fire station. Unfortunately, traditional InfoSec strategy is like a fire station attempting to prevent any fires from happening in their district. The fire station tells citizens to wear

PPE, to never use anything potentially flammable, and to follow a complicated set of procedures based on the premise of fire prevention being the most important goal in their lives. Complicated fire safety rules discourage healthy new construction, choking the potential for vital community growth. When fires do occur, the fire station scolds any citizens involved, but also demands that citizens proactively tell them about any potential fire hazards —not the best incentive scheme.

Security Chaos Engineering, in contrast, is more like the fire stations we know today (but with some cool enhancements). The fire station focuses on their ability to quickly and gracefully respond to fires, attempting to minimize damage. These security chaos firefighters conduct drills to gain muscle memory of responding to incidents, injecting failures like a hose leaking or doors being inaccessible to learn from them and improve their processes.

With more confidence in our firefighting abilities, we can shift focus to designing less flammable structures, working in partnership with local builders and officials to ensure that appropriate attention is paid to minimizing the impact of fires from the beginning. It is collaborative, constructive, and continuous—resulting in a much more resilient community than a fire station attempting to enforce punitive measures that make life more difficult for the citizens whose lives they're supposed to protect.

It cannot remain information security against the world. Security Chaos Engineering is a path forward for InfoSec to support safe community growth and be proud of the tangible outcomes that result.

The Solid Impact of Soft Skills

Kim Z. Dale

Early in my career, a boss reprimanded me for being too calm. My calmness wasn't exactly the problem. The true problem was my calm reaction to someone else's lack of calmness and how that was perceived.

One of our key systems was down. I talked to the people who were actively working on it and was assured they understood the issue and how to resolve it. I was confident they would get the system back as quickly as possible. There wasn't anything more I could personally do to help (or so I thought).

I returned to my office to work on other things when a *big important manager* whose team was *highly impacted* by the outage came in raging. Wanting to know *what's going on*?! Wanting to know *when will it be fixed?!* Wanting to know *why wasn't i doing anything about it?!*

I calmly (too calmly) told him the problem was being taken care of, which he interpreted as me being dismissive of his concerns. (To be fair, I probably was a tad dismissive. After all, people were working on the issue, and I had other things to do!) After a few choice expletives, he stormed off to complain about me to my boss who then summoned me to her office to yell at me about upsetting the manager.

For a while, I misinterpreted the moral of this story. I initially thought the lesson to be learned was to be sure to act sufficiently frenzied when there is a problem in order to show you grasp the seriousness of the situation, but of course, that's not the real lesson. What I now know I should have done in that moment was let the guy rant. And listen to him rant. Really listen to him. Empathize with his concerns. Make him feel heard. Perhaps I would have realized there was something I could do to help. At a minimum, I would have been far less likely to damage my relationship with a powerful manager and get in trouble with my boss. (I did not remain in that role for long.)

Information security professionals often complain other people don't listen to us when we tell them all the *very important things* they should *do* or *not do* in order to keep systems secure, but how often do we really listen to those other people? How much do we work to understand needs and priorities outside of information security? Listening and empathy are not only good for relationship building—listening and empathy are powerful tools for designing and gaining adoption for information security solutions.

When information security folks talk to non-InfoSec folks, we tend to prattle on about what we need from them (Don't click on things! Don't download things! Don't reuse passwords! Don't write down passwords!), not thinking about the fact that the people we are talking to have their own stuff to worry about. But if we take the time to understand those other people's needs and priorities we can better communicate how our work supports theirs. And if our information security priorities do not align with the priorities of the business and our clients, there is something wrong.

Technology professionals often belittle things like listening and empathy as "soft skills," but these skills can be hard, very hard, to hone for those who don't take to them naturally. The effort is worth it though. The most effective information security people I know balance technical expertise and people skills. To be a better information security professional, learn to listen to people outside our profession and care about what they say. You'll learn a lot.

What Is Good Cyber Hygiene Within Information Security?

Lauren Zink

Everyone has a daily routine that they follow that is unique to them and typically includes maintaining personal hygiene throughout some aspect of their day. Security hygiene must be just as important as the personal hygiene that everyone already practices (or should) day in and day out. One of the biggest threats to a company can be their people, and not necessarily in a malicious way, but typically just by being negligent or not knowing better due to never being taught good security habits in the first place. This is why decent cyber hygiene is imperative at all levels of the organization and should be a main priority of the security team.

Solid hygiene in information security needs to be incorporated into all aspects of the security program from people to processes and even technology. No shortcuts should be taken, and it must never be assumed that tools and technology alone can protect an organization. A multilayered approach that incorporates governance and compliance as well as security training and awareness into everyday security operations in all of its facets is truly the best approach when it comes to securing an organization, its people, and its assets.

Oftentimes, there may be employees such as those on the technology teams or even the executives that may think they should be exempt from continued security training and awareness. However, it is vital to remember and remind them often that they also have targets on their back, sometimes even more so than other groups or people. Cyber best practices need to be performed and demonstrated from the security team first and foremost so a team can truly say they practice what they preach. It should also be exhibited from the top down to demonstrate to all employees in an organization what should be emulated from the bottom up as well.

Also, cyber hygiene needs to be practiced not only at work, but also at home. Being vigilant when it comes to security matters can have a positive impact in all aspects of a person's life. When security training encompasses topics that people face in their daily personal lives, it can not only play an important role in keeping them safe at home, but also help create overall remarkable security habits. And when security shifts from being seen as a requirement to a natural and thought-free habit is when a person feels enabled to make good secure decisions both at work and at home.

What this really comes down to is the company continually educating their workforce on the risks and how employees can play their role and feel empowered when it comes to protecting the company. Start with the security basics, develop a healthy baseline understanding of the risks, and build from there. Help your employees create good cyber habits and routines by providing a wide variety of training and awareness opportunities tailored specifically to their security wants and needs.

The risks companies face due to cyber incidents are why more and more companies need to deploy strong security awareness programs as a preventative and multilayered measure in addition to policies and technology that are already in place. I'm hopeful that the importance of having a robust security awareness program with a dedicated person and/or team that is employed to create solid cyber hygiene among employees will continue to gain traction as the risk of the human element is not going anywhere and needs to be educated, engaged, and protected.

Phishing

Lauren Zink

Phishing is currently the most common form of digital social engineering, which is when someone tries to make a person perform an action or provide specific information they are soliciting through various means. Phishing more specifically is when an email is sent with malicious intent with the appearance of coming from a legitimate person or company. However, there are typically some red flags that should alert a receiver that the email is indeed nefarious, but not always.

The effectiveness of a simple phishing email can be shocking and eye opening to employees and the company. Usually, a phishing email will include a fraudulent link or an attachment. This is how the attacker is going to infiltrate the network to gain information about the receiver or the company. However, that is not always the case. Some emails may not include any links or attachments but may just be trying to solicit general information or get the receiver to complete an action.

Some general information that a phishing email may try to solicit includes personal or company information such as usernames, passwords, or other personally identifiable information (PII). The email may also ask for contact information directly related to other people within your company, bank routing information, or even IP address information. The email could even go as far as to impersonate or spoof other people within your company to get the receiver to be more apt to provide the information they are trying to obtain by preying on vulnerabilities and the innate instinct that people just want to help.

Phishing can be a rather simple and easy attack vector which can go something like this:

1. A single employee clicks a link in an email.
2. That link is set up to perform credential harvesting.

3. This action could then also enable a series of other events to occur that could result in a significant data breach.

4. The cost of the data breach could be incredibly high and could affect individuals that played no role in the actions taken within the email.

Some phishing emails may have some rather apparent red flags including, but not limited to, poor grammar, strange sender or domain, or not coming from a company or person you have ever communicated with before. Other emails may not be as obvious as others in sending off the instant vibe that it is malicious. Luckily there are various security tools as well as training available to help assist with identifying phishing emails or preventing them from getting to your employees in the first place. This multilayered approach to email security is a solid line of defense.

Because phishing is occurring at such an alarming rate and has been for years with no indication of slowing down, it is imperative that companies focus on phishing awareness and education as a high priority within their security program. It is also important that phishing tests be a part of a larger security awareness program that also includes training and education on a multitude of topics. This is an effective way to give employees a real, hands-on training experience to see how they would react to a real phishing attempt and will also allow information to be gathered regarding how well-educated employees are on phishing in the first place. If your employees don't know what to do when they receive a suspicious email or how and who to report it to, train them on this information and then provide a phishing test to assess their knowledge along with supplemental training material and communications delivered through various avenues all year long.

Building a New Security Program

Lauren Zink

Building a new security program, no matter the focus, is not an easy task. Although it may be a heavy lift, there are several things one can do to help make the task a bit less daunting while ensuring overall prolonged success. Instead of thinking big picture, start by thinking a bit smaller, which is much less intimidating and easier to digest. This can be accomplished by developing a program that is broken down into smaller segments with short-term plans that will help organically develop a long-term plan and program.

A breakdown of some considerations when developing a new security program may include the following:

1. Understand your current foundation.
2. Develop a solid plan.
3. Engage stakeholders and employees.
4. Communicate and implement the program.
5. Develop metrics and measure the effectiveness of the program.
6. Be prepared for roadblocks and shifts in the initial plan.
7. Continually revisit and update the program plan and clearly communicate progress and changes.

Within the first 30 days, start by getting to know the teams, building relationships, and understanding the current state of affairs of the security program and the business. Meet with leadership and discuss the plan to ensure everyone is on the same page regarding their expectations for the program from day one. Make it a point to document everything, not only for your leadership, but also for yourself. This will ensure that there is a clear visual of what needs be achieved within the first month.

Next is a 90-day plan, which is still in the beginning stages of program development, but offers enough time to demonstrate a few accomplishments and/or a vision for the potential future state of the program. Now is a good time to start communicating the plan and garnering feedback from stakeholders before fully implementing the program.

Naturally, next in line would be the one-year plan, which demonstrates what the program owner and leadership hope to accomplish within the first year. With a few months of progress in the books it may be a good timeframe to review what metrics can begin to be measured to help demonstrate the effectiveness of the program in its current state as well as stretch goals to improve said metrics.

Following the one-year plan, start to think big picture and how to create an impact with the new security program within the business in the first three years. Consider ways to continue to refine, update, and expand the current security offerings in place after year one.

Once all the ideas are in place for the 30-day to three-year plans, organize them in a way that is easily accessible and effective for collaboration with your team. Create a working document so all stakeholders can refer back to the plan while documenting progress and any roadblocks along the way. This plan may also be useful going forward to demonstrate where there are gaps in the program and where extra support and resources are needed. A good visual of the plan can also be utilized by leadership to demonstrate the roadmap for the security plan to the business. Remember, the plan is a fluid document that adjusts to the needs of employees and the business and reflects the current risks that need to be addressed, so ensure it is continually updated and communicated.

Finally, aim to make the program more mature and effective, while ensuring that it demonstrates growth year after year. Always keep an open mind to changing and updating the program so that it can be effective in enabling the business and making the workplace more secure.

Using Isolation Zones to Increase Cloud Security

Lee Atchison

In cloud-based infrastructure architectures, as it is in on-premise infrastructure architectures, it's generally considered best practice for security purposes to split your infrastructure into zones. These zones provide levels of security isolation that keep your application data and core capabilities safer from outside attacks.

General Isolation Zone Architecture

A good best practice for zone isolation is to split your backend infrastructure into three distinct isolation zones. Typically, the three zones are:

Public zone
> This zone is exposed to and connected to the internet. IP addresses in this zone are generally publicly accessible from the internet. Servers, while generally protected via various security firewalls, receive traffic directly from users out in the internet.

Demilitarized zone (DMZ)
> This zone is isolated from the internet and is set up so that only specific servers—those in the public zone—have the ability to send traffic to them. End users, out in the internet wild, have no access to these servers.

Internal zone
> This zone is further isolated from the internet. No publicly facing servers, even application servers such as those running "frontend services," have the ability to send traffic to this zone. Only servers isolated in the DMZ, and servers within the application backend, have the ability to communicate with servers in the internal zone.

This infrastructure architecture can best be visualized as follows:

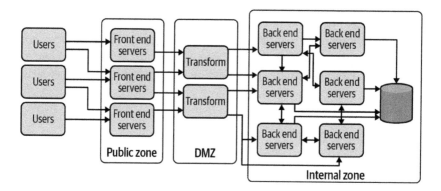

Managing Communications Flow

In the image, you can see the user on the far left, in the wild of the internet, talking to the application frontend services. These services are located in the *public zone*, which is exposed and visible to the internet. These services—and everything located in the public zone—must be hardened against all ranges of cyberattacks. Typically, the frontend services perform the bare essential capabilities of the application—only those things that need to be handled at the very front. This typically includes account verification, authentication, authorization, load balancing, traffic shedding, etc.

These frontend services talk to transition services located in the *DMZ*, or *demilitarized zone*. This zone is a buffer between the frontend (public zone) and the backend (internal zone). For security purposes, only services specifically located in the public zone are allowed to talk to services in the DMZ. No end user can communicate directly from the public internet with services in the DMZ. Services in the DMZ typically perform translational and transitional processes, converting calls from frontend services to calls that can be executed by backend services.

These DMZ transition services call the appropriate backend services in the *internal zone*, or *backend zone*. Here, in the heart of the application, services can talk freely amongst themselves, but they only accept commands and traffic that arrive from the transition services in the DMZ. Services in the internal zone have private IP addresses that are not directly accessible from the internet. They do not accept requests that come from the public zone, nor directly from end users.

These zones create safety shields that help isolate traffic from the public internet and prevent mistakes or errors in internal services from accidentally allowing traffic from the public internet to have unfettered access to the backend. Only requests that have been properly vetted by the frontend services, properly processed through the DMZ transition services, can make it to the backend. This triple buffer provides a significant level of system security.

If It's Remembered for You, Forensics Can Uncover It

Lodrina Cherne

Our phones and computers aim to be more user friendly with every app and operating system upgrade, remembering the person you email the most, the file you recently opened, or the website you always visit. Because this tracking data makes devices more user friendly, it also means that forensic examiners have an increasing amount of data to draw from when investigating digital crime scenes.

If your device recommends doing something you've done before, these remembered actions are something that can be uncovered by a digital forensics examiner. By identifying what your devices remember, you'll be better prepared to work with a forensic professional. Digital forensics and incident response (DFIR) is a field that involves figuring out what happened on a system or network after it happens. Here's just a few examples of what our computers and mobile devices remember for us that forensics can recover:

- Ever open your word processing app and see it recommend the last 10 files you worked on as things you might want to open again? Forensics can tell you when you opened those files.

- Scroll through your open apps on a mobile device and see previews of those applications as you were last using them? The screenshots are recoverable by forensic analysis.

- Do you like viewing your *Downloads* folder as a list of files but your *Pictures* folder as icons showing little previews of photos? That your computer remembers which settings you have for different folders means it remembers what folders you've been in—even if you don't open any files in those locations!

Think about these examples of things remembered for you and you'll find many more. For example, I have a unique name that a new phone or spell-checker wouldn't know out of the box. Once I teach my phone that I don't want to underline my name with red squiggly lines indicating a spelling error, it will remember my name as a word in a custom dictionary. This means it's stored and remembered in some database and yes—forensics can recover custom dictionaries too!

When you've identified a scenario that could use forensics, a word of warning: performing this kind of analysis should be performed by a DFIR specialist trained in preserving and analyzing digital evidence. Even if you have the authority to browse through a device, you may be performing the digital equivalent of trampling through a crime scene by taking a peek.

When you've identified that a DFIR examiner can help you out, here are things to do in a corporate environment in tandem with engaging a forensic professional:

- Coordinate with your legal team and make sure your IT, security, and executive teams are in the loop.

- Identify your key dates and systems involved; once you've identified the systems, don't use them! The universe of data a forensic examiner might want can include computers, mobile devices, email, cloud and file shares, chat logs, and removable devices.

- Place an eDiscovery or litigation hold on relevant mailboxes. This is one way to retain email data while getting ready to export the most complete collection of email possible.

After preserving data you've identified, a forensics professional is also best suited to give context to that data, especially if that information might go to court. Often it's not enough to say that an important file was found on a system. Forensics can add context around when the file was created, downloaded, copied, or emailed.

Whether you're investigating a crime, pursuing legal action, or wondering what an attacker did after breaking into your network, being able to identify digital evidence can help make a case for what happened. By observing what's remembered on your devices as you go about your day, you're now empowered to understand what data might be recovered by a professional examiner in an investigation.

Certifications Considered Harmful

Louis Nyffenegger

Certifications are becoming a shortcut for people who can afford them and a barrier for people who cannot.

As of 2020, we have seen an explosion in the number of certifications. A few organizations are fighting hard to get the top spot and the industry recognition and money that come with them. Certifications have also become the ultimate gate for hiring managers. A few letters in your resume can make the difference between whether it gets read or not, leaving a lot of people who cannot afford certifications behind.

As someone providing training, it is straightforward to recognize the impact certifications have on a global scale. If you get to talk to people from countries where getting a US$1,000 certification represents an annual salary, you will quickly understand the issue. People coming from privileged backgrounds can boast about "trying harder" while the rest feel left out. Content sharing in our industry allows anyone to get from zero to hero on their own. Even if you cannot afford training, you can get most ingredients and the recipes. There is no secret sauce. Training platforms are just a catalyst in your learning journey. On the other end, you just cannot get certified unless you pay the price.

And the price is not only a dollar figure during checkout. The amount of time it takes to prepare and pass such exams is a huge sink. You can forget passing most exams if you are a single parent or lack a good support network. Certifications are thus widening the gap created by discrimination. "How come this person didn't get their previous manager to pay for this certification?" one may ask themself before picking the person with the certifications who may not have been subject to discrimination. Personal and financial pressures caused people to pick the easy way out—some cheated on exams. A quick fix was introduced: proctoring, making certifications even harder for many. Those few lucky enough to obtain scholarships reinforce the whole phenomenon: "People can get this certification if they really want it."

Having gone through all this effort, the lucky ones still managing to get certifications, perhaps while dealing with emotional and financial stress, quickly understand. Despite being the ultimate HR requirement, most technical people don't care about certifications. They laughed at some or believe others are just not indicative of a candidate's skill set, leaving some candidates in debt and disappointed.

You may ask, what can I do? While the problem may be too big and too far gone to tackle as an individual, like the issue of climate change, it helps if everyone does just a bit. First, if you're advertising a role, don't require certifications for applicants. You are just missing talent. You may "value diversity," but your prerequirements scream otherwise. "Only males applied for this role" says the person who has never heard about the confidence gap and required few certifications. Don't put your certifications next to your name on professional networks. After all, you don't introduce yourself to people as "John Doe, CABC, CDEF" when you meet them. Finally, stop recommending certifications to people just because it's an easy answer—instead, tell them to learn the basics and then aim for depth or breadth. Avoid shortcuts; it's a journey, not a sprint. People can enjoy getting certified, but this should not be just another gatekeeping mechanism.

Security Considerations for IoT Device Management

Mansi Thakar

There are constantly new additions to the environment, whether it's at your work or home. From Alexas to smart toasters to the remote sensors that track how many people walked through the hallway, these Internet of Things (IoT) devices are being incorporated at an exponentially fast rate. This article aims to expand on security requirements with respect to the IoT device management life cycle.

Approved IoT devices and internal IoT development

Considerations about whether your devices should be manageable from a central platform, whether there is a security review board that looks at the device from both a functionality and an architectural point of view, and how often do you want to review the device can be explored here.

Inventory

There is more than just one type of owner for such devices. For example, there would be someone responsible for the device itself. If it's an in-house made device, then this person can be the creator of it. There could be a solution owner, someone who is responsible for meeting the business unit's requirements. Depending on which tool you choose to track, collecting more information than less is helpful.

Here are a few items, not an exhaustive list:

- Manufacturer and model
- Owner(s)
- Installation location and photograph of the device at installation (this can help with future audits)
- Device status (active, inactive, decommissioned)

- Firmware information (latest version, last date it was updated)
- Data collection and classification

Device and data. Security considerations such as having minimum open ports and network microsegmentation where appropriate are vital when understanding how this device will connect to the network. Minimal data storage requirements, what kind of data can be collected, and how it will be transmitted are again vital questions to answer especially as it relates to legal and privacy requirements.

Maintenance and testing. How often is the device updated (firmware and OS)? How often will it be scanned for vulnerabilities? How is it scanned for vulnerabilities? If it's a third-party device, is there enough language in the contracts to provide insight into the roles and responsibilities? Does the device have logging and a monitoring capability? Is there removable storage capability?

Decommissioning/disposal. This is often overlooked. As much as onboarding a device is important, offboarding is of equal if not even more importance. Who is responsible for device disposal? How will it be disposed of?

Physical security and digital authentication. Who has access to the device? What kind of authentication requirements are in place? Are there default passwords that need to be changed? How is this audited? Is multifactor authentication a possibility?

Though this is not an exhaustive list of requirements, the baseline is to identify what the device does, why does it need to do it, how does it do it, and most importantly who is responsible for it.

Lessons Learned: Cybersecurity Road Trip

Mansi Thakar

Over the span of 26 days, I traveled 3,600 miles in a bright green RV to interview 15 trailblazers as part of a PBS documentary, *Life Hackers*. Here are a few snippets from the trip, to keep you going even when the road is less traveled.

Myth Versus Reality

Our first interview was with Christina Morillo, the author of this book! A question that was near to my heart was regarding balance. It has been a common theme in my life—whether it's balancing two different cultures or two different fields of study. Her reply to how to achieve balance, especially since cybersecurity isn't a 9-to-5 job, was simply, "Balance is BS." There was no such thing as achieving balance; Morillo's perspective was that you have to prioritize and compromise.

Unleash Your Growth

As the youngest in my graduate program where most others come with 30+ years of experience (I haven't even lived 30 years on this planet yet), I often feel a bit of a wall between myself and them. However, Rohan Amin, the CISO of JP Morgan Chase and Co., shed light that with persistence and truly developing a niche for yourself, everything else comes into line. He continued to say that cybersecurity is a field of problem solving, so pick a problem and immerse yourself into it.

Michael Echols, former Director at the US Department of Homeland Security, provided a different perspective on this perceived wall of mine. He said sometimes you may feel like something is holding your hand back from grabbing the apple you want; however, if you look closely enough it might be your other hand holding your hand back. We are sometimes the biggest obstacle and hindrance to our own growth.

Lisa Jiggetts, founder of the Women's Society of Cyberjutsu, echoed similar sentiments: "What's the worst that can happen? You will get a no. But you learn and get ready for the next one."

When the going gets tough, here is what analyst Ben Brown's wife said to him (and me): "I'm not laying a brick, I'm building a cathedral." Such a handy line to help keep the bigger perspective in mind.

A part of me was never truly comfortable switching from the life science field to the world of computers. Would I have to forgo the hours spent understanding the synthesis of alkenes to better understand how the AES algorithm works? Through interactions with leaders, the answer was revealed to be: no! So many of the leaders we conversed with came from all sorts of varying paths such as anthropology, psychology, philosophy, economics, education, etc. And each found a way to make a niche for themselves by combining their previous fields with cybersecurity.

Finding Your Voice

Maresa Vermulst

Within an organization, it can be difficult to find your voice. There are many different styles of communication; people operate at different levels within an organization with their own priorities and lingo. Besides, we all have our prejudices and biases. Especially when pressure builds, these differences in communication can become a major factor in building frustration between people.

Miscommunication can cause detrimental effects on relationships within the team and have negative effects on projects (flaws, missed improvements because ideas were not heard, etc.) but also have a big impact on your own well-being and mental health. Having nobody to hear you can make you feel powerless. This can be a contributing factor for burnout.

How can you make yourself heard within an organization or in a team? Does it feel sometimes like you must yell before other people take notice of you?

Over the years people have shared some practical tips with me that I now, in turn, would like to share with you:

Learn their language.

Every department has its own lingo. When trying to communicate a data breach to someone from marketing, for example, emphasize the effect this can have on brand image. Don't go into technical details or possible legal ramifications; *start with what is relevant for their field.*

When voicing your concerns to C-levels point out that a project doesn't align with the business goals. Some companies place great worth on their core values. Use these terms when pitching your idea.

You can also explain something in the context of a subject someone is familiar with. For example, a neurologist explained to me that she can only test for hardware issues in the brain. We currently have no way to test for software issues. Especially when it comes to highly complex subjects, analogies like these can be useful to get a point across.

Find allies.

Look for people within different departments you can level with, share tips with, or just have a fun chat with. If you get stuck, ask if they know someone who can help with your issue (and assist them by doing the same for them). This can create short communication lines that are helpful when dealing with issues, especially when the workload is high. It can cut through layers of bureaucracy. Just use this responsibly; don't make a highway out of a shortcut.

Find a mediator.

Sometimes you just can't seem to get the message across. Irrespective of the reason for this, a quick solution can be to ask someone you know to get the message across for you. Or you can ask for a moment of their time to help you by giving you pointers. It can be as simple as having a third party look over a mail conversation that is getting nowhere or that frustrates you (don't do that with confidential mails though).

Practice your skills.

Practice getting your point across in a presentation, blog post, or your next meeting. If you feel comfortable, film yourself while presenting or watch yourself in a mirror and pay attention to your posture, intonation, and speech rate. Watch presenters as they cover a subject and how public speakers emphasize points. You don't have to become a master at presenting or even present to others. The goal is to practice, to become more comfortable in a situation where you want to clarify your position or opinion to others.

Best Practices with Vulnerability Management

Mari Galloway

Vulnerability management (VM) is on everyone's mind, but most don't know how to successfully implement and maintain a fully functional program. It's more than just having tools in place and running scans. Vulnerability management is the cyclical process of identifying, categorizing, prioritizing, remediating, and mitigating software vulnerabilities.

For new organizations and old ones referencing the CIS Top 20 Basic Security Controls, you see that VM is the third control on that list after identifying all your assets and software. This means, before any penetration testing or implementation of other controls, you MUST identify your systems and the vulnerabilities first. This will drive the rest of your controls as you are able to see what is critical and what should be remediated or mitigated to improve your security posture.

Here are four best practices for successfully implementing and maintaining a vulnerability management program:

Have a dedicated team.
> This may seem like a no-brainer, having two or three people to dedicate time and energy to this entire process. But some organizations may leave the VM process to the security operations team, who are already swamped with alerts. Having a dedicated team not only allows the organization to tackle this process effectively, but also gives the cyber team the opportunity to build relationships with the various stakeholders, thus achieving more timely remediation and mitigation.

Identify the crown jewels.

Next you need to identify your systems and categorize them based on the data that they hold and the value of that data should it be breached. This is vital as it allows you to use your time effectively and efficiently on remediation. It makes absolutely no sense to run a scan, gather the vulnerabilities, and then send over 3,000 critical vulnerabilities to be fixed. It won't happen and the other teams won't be happy.

Invest in scanning programs.

This is the kicker, having the means to scan two devices or thousands of devices. Investing in tools will make this process so much easier. They allow you to schedule scans to occur during less critical times, reducing the need for downtime. These tools also store the data and track trends to show success with remediation. Various types of reports can be generated from tools that can be used by everyone from the tech to upper management to make decisions. Tools now also incorporate threat intel from hundreds of sources to help prioritize remediation.

Relationships are a must.

Probably the MOST important part of this is building a relationship with the folks who will be fixing the issues as well as their leadership team. This is how you get the work done. This also allows you to showcase successes to the teams that are doing the work. The cyber team can also provide additional value by assisting the teams with remediation and mitigation and providing additional input into fixing some of the issues.

Remember that the VM process is a continuous process and must be nurtured for true success. There must be buy-in from all parties to move remediation along and get things done.

Social Engineering

Marina Ciavatta

You may have never heard the term "social engineering" before, but you surely have had contact with it, by watching a spy or heist movie, or maybe reading about fraudsters or even suffering because of scammers. You don't need to go through the headache of identity theft to know how much damage social engineering can cause if used in a malicious way by criminals.

Social engineering is a set of skills and techniques related to exploitation and analysis of human behavior. The goal is to provoke or take advantage of "human error." This means that the social engineer studies their targets, learning how they behave and exploring their reactions to achieve objectives.

Humans obey commands and have behavior patterns related to the system they live in, a clear parallel on how machines are programmed. The social engineer is able to understand and break this process down, just like a hacker looks for security flaws to exploit. It's no surprise that social engineering is also known as "human hacking."

Goals may vary: extracting or stealing confidential data, sabotage or spying, breaking and entering restricted areas, and so forth. The attacks list is even bigger. The most popular ones are based on the "baiting" technique, which is to attract the victim's attention. Special promos you can't pass on, benefits (quid pro quo), unexpected prizes…everything that is shiny, luring the prey.

Emotional manipulation is also sprinkled in almost every social engineering attack, inducing the victim to take impulsive actions without questioning. In many cases it is disguised as an alleged bank or credit card alert, a "security" notification, or even using the names of trusted people and companies.

All a criminal needs is a click (phishing). They need a target that won't pay attention to what they're downloading and have no suspicions about the form asking for their valuable information—such as a login and password. They need the victim to believe everything the voice over the phone is saying, especially if they're creating a problem out of thin air just to provide the solution a few minutes later.

It's important to highlight that social engineering is one of the top information security concerns nowadays. Some of the most critical incidents from the past decade have been ignited due to human flaws being explored, for example, having an infiltrator in the company (insider threat) or a "harmless" call and email from the support team (pretexting).

Social engineering has many forms and names, just like its agents. It explores something that's eternally hard to protect and no security system on the planet, no matter how sophisticated, is sufficient to shield from human behavior. After all, everyone has their weak spot—and it's the social engineer's job to study them.

Of course it's scary. But social engineering can—and should be—used for the greater good, just as any other hacking skill. It's about how to turn knowledge into a defense tool. It's about spreading awareness regarding the attacks and techniques to make people confident enough to stand up to it, to question, to confront, and even to use it in their favor—to make people talk about security so everyone can understand its value, including themselves.

We should never stop talking about social engineering and exploring it, showing others that no matter how cruel a scammer can be, our true strength lies in what we do and what we are; our behaviors are not just "flaws and weaknesses." They are the essence of the human element transformation, from the weakest link to the strongest one.

Stalkerware: When Malware and Domestic Abuse Coincide

Martijn Grooten

Stalkerware, also sometimes called "spouseware," is defined by the Coalition Against Stalkerware as software, made available directly to individuals, that enables a remote user to monitor the activities on another user's device without that user's consent and without explicit, persistent notification to that user in a manner that may facilitate intimate partner surveillance, harassment, abuse, stalking, and/or violence.

Stalkerware is functionally similar to spyware. One important difference though is that it is typically installed manually by someone with (temporary) access to a device, whereas ordinary spyware, like most malware, is installed remotely, either through an exploit or through social engineering. This means stalkerware doesn't need to try hard to bypass security restrictions as they could be turned off during the manual installation process.

From a traditional digital security point of view, stalkerware seems easy to defend against. After all, you wouldn't give a cybercriminal or a nation state actor access to your phone. But these aren't the kind of actors using stalkerware: the typical person using stalkerware is an abusive partner or ex-partner. They often have such access or can obtain it through force or social engineering.

This main use of stalkerware is not what vendors want you to believe from their shiny websites, where they talk about their software being ideal tools for parents to monitor their children's online behavior. Indeed, legitimate parental control software exists but, crucially, is installed with explicit consent and doesn't hide its presence from the phone user. Really, there is no need for a stealthy "spy app" to monitor your children's behavior. Unless of course it's not really your children you want to monitor. References to their use in relationships, if present at all, are often very hidden, such as an explanation of how the app purchase shows up on a credit card bill, or the suggestion that the app will help you detect if "they"—the children?—are cheating.

Though stalkerware hides itself well, a security expert will probably be able to find and remove the apps from the device without much difficulty. And should this fail to work, there is always the option of a factory reset.

But approaching stalkerware this way can be unwise and even dangerous: the abuser will likely notice the removal of the app, and this can—and in practice regularly does—make the abuse escalate. It is thus important to give the survivor full agency: maybe they think it's safer for the stalkerware to remain installed and to adapt their behavior instead. Or maybe they want to wait until they have a safety plan.

And there is another thing to consider: though stalkerware has gotten a lot of media attention recently, it is not the only way in which technology is used to enable abusive relationships. Other examples include tools that, though knowledge of the password, scrape iCloud backups, (legitimate) location tracking apps, or simply a shared password that is used to check emails or messages.

Though it is very important to take the stories of domestic abuse survivors seriously, it is also important to keep in mind they may not be correct in their technical analysis of the situation: it may not be stalkerware, or it may be stalkerware and also something else. Thus, take a holistic approach when helping someone in such a situation.

And never forget that first and foremost you are dealing with a possibly traumatized abuse survivor. No matter your technical expertise, that should always be central in your approach.

Understanding and Exploring Risk

Dr. Meg Layton

One thing InfoSec professionals should know is how to consider and effectively discuss risk within their environment. Risk is often explored using a common framework or set of steps: identify your assets and then identify threats and vulnerabilities to those assets. Once these are enumerated, consider the impacts that may occur should threats or vulnerabilities become a reality, and then those impacts are explored against the likelihood of that impact actually occurring. Understanding this framework means that one needs to enumerate the risks for an organization and discuss the implications of threats within the organizational context.

It is essential to understand the organizational context when it comes to risk because it is not the same and varies from organization to organization. Much like my threat model is not the same as your threat model, my organizational tolerance for risk is not the same as your organization's tolerance.

In a study conducted a few years ago by ISACA, most respondents said that the biggest skill gap in today's security professionals is the *ability to understand the business*. This is the same when discussing vulnerabilities, threats, and risks: if one does not understand its impact, one does not understand. The latest threat may be interesting from a technological perspective, and it may be interesting from a news perspective, but if it does not impact the business and represents minimal risk, there is not much time to be spent on it.

If you learn of a threat that impacts an operating system and it is very severe, does it matter if you do not run that operating system within your organization? You may take a sweep through to confirm that nothing is missed, but you don't spend any time worrying. It's a tree in a forest that fell without a sound. On the other hand, if you have the correct operating system in your environment, you now are in the position to explain either your mitigations (why this might not matter because of additional steps that you have taken) or your required action (why you need the team to conduct an emergency patch). These conversations are served well when they are bound by the organizational context and implications of the threat. It is very important that the conversation moves from the general news hysteria to actual organizational impact. For example, thousands of web servers around the world may translate to two web servers within your organization, hosting specific applications, vital to your business. That's where the organizational focus should be.

You may find your organization takes one of three different responses:

1. They may choose to reduce the risk or avoid the risk. This is the typical response if the patch is to be applied.

2. They may decide to transfer the risk if insurance companies or third-party providers are involved.

3. They may either accept the risk or reject the risk. This is the hardest thing for InfoSec professionals: if you have appropriately advocated the risk, the organization may still choose to say, "That's OK, we still don't want to address it right now." This is frequently due to the organization accepting the loss that is associated with the potential risk and is common in organizations with competing priorities.

Many organizational decisions start with considering risk and evaluating the impact of that risk. Knowing how to discuss, defend, and apply organizational context around risk allows you to have robust conversations about the security of your organization and develop a trusted voice as an InfoSec professional.

The Psychology of Incident Response

Melanie Ensign

One of the most commonly overlooked aspects of effective incident response (IR) is the intellectual and practical mastery of self-regulating our reactions as individuals and organizations. In particular, many IR plans fail to consider the necessary steps to avoid, minimize, or recover from a state of panic within the security team or surrounding stakeholders such as executives, regulators, and customers.

Avoiding Panic

When we are panicked, we are unable to self-regulate effectively. This is because when panicked, the brain's ability to consume and process large amounts of information is temporarily suspended as resources are diverted to reflexive and instinctive behaviors. Knowing how to avoid or minimize panic is important for ensuring the decisions we make and actions we take in the wake of a security incident are appropriate and productive for both short-term and long-term objectives.

Panic often reflects a gap in *readiness*. Whether technical, procedural, or relational, these gaps exist between the actual demands of an incident and the organization's current skills, tools, and preparedness.

Anticipating Stakeholder Readiness

It's not only a security team's readiness that matters, but also each of their stakeholder's ability to regulate emotional and physical reactions that impacts how well they can direct and sustain attention on the most important aspects of an incident. If they've never been exposed to an incident or your specific process, they'll be less likely to self-regulate effectively, which increases the potential for panic. There's nothing like a panicked executive to throw a wrench in an otherwise carefully designed response.

Learning how to follow procedures is one way to remind everyone what they should be looking for during an incident—and the best way to do this is to design incident response plans as an extension of day-to-day operations rather than something that is only used for major incidents that occur less frequently. You want your plan to be used as often as possible because as tasks become more familiar, they require less conscious attention, and associated skills become embedded in our memory, demanding less cognitive capacity. Practicing a procedure also helps reduce delays in action due to uncertainty about what to deal with first.

Teaching Stakeholders to Self-Regulate

Every day, security teams have the opportunity to increase the ability of all relevant parties to effectively self-regulate and avoid panic. In fact, understanding the psychology of incidents should motivate security professionals to engage in more proactive, more frequent, and more productive communications with executives, regulators, customers, and industry peers on an ongoing basis to increase their familiarity with your specific incident response procedures.

Keeping everyone around you focused on the right things is one of the most challenging aspects of incident response, but it is critical to achieving productive outcomes. Fortunately, being able to consciously self-regulate is a skill that can be learned, practiced, and refined among security teams as well as stakeholder groups—but only if you start early and often. Remember, once panic sets in, the brain's most discerning cognitive abilities are put on hold.

Priorities and Ethics/Morality

Michael Weber

Be sure to protect yourself. There have been great ethical hackers that have toed the line and landed in some deep life-destroying trouble from various institutions. Legal and civil penalties have been levied against many notable individuals with one that always comes to mind: Aaron Swartz. If you do not know the case, look it up. Aaron is just one individual on a long list that dates back all the way to phone phreaking that tried to change the world, and got caught. Intellectual property law, various cybercrime initiatives, and national security laws have made much of what InfoSec people do two sides of the very same coin. You always hear black hat, white hat, or even the notorious gray hat, but I am here to tell you that there is more at risk to us than you may think.

InfoSec is just one field that is attacked on a daily basis, and if you ever get to find one of those "great security vulnerabilities" in some large corporation, you will understand what I mean. To an entity like that, the law is more important than the security. They could sit on that vulnerability forever. Make note of the folks that publish without regard; you may see their talks suppressed, their travel restricted, and their lives ruined. I highlight this issue as a legitimate warning to those who participate. I also mention this because anonymity is at a price today. I will not even spend a second describing the methods and entities that track almost every digital transaction globally. Whether corporate or government: Watch Out. I am not telling you to go hack the Gibson here. I am just advising you that in some situations having a lawyer and remaining anonymous until the time is right might be a great decision.

Everyone does it. Everyone lawyers up, and you should too if the time comes. You have rights, and just because generations upon generations of people do not understand how technology works, you should not be at a disadvantage. You should also help us fight to create, and support anonymous technologies, no matter what reasons the ignorant may bring to the table to thwart the efforts of the folks that day in and day out work on that code that keeps more people than we can imagine safe. All of this matters now more than ever as the internet continues to be centralized, and kill switches and walls are inserted into our global networks. As time goes on please remember and look back to the generations that fought before you did. Remember that they had MORE freedom than you have today. Remember that there was LESS law than we have today. While some of these freedoms have been stolen in the name of many initiatives to keep the world, some laws have been created to protect you, and just because they are shrugged off by groups and figures as not applicable to you does not mean that they are.

A strong moral sense is never mentioned in a job interview, and never even really mentioned in a NDA. It is because morals are a human invention, and in an age where digital trust is being eroded, we should lean into those morals even more. To some that may mean lobbying inside of an organization to do the right thing and secure things correctly. To some, anonymity is the only way. To others that may mean you need to break laws to change them in countries/places where even owning a computer is illegal. Whoever you are, stay safe.

DevSecOps: Continuous Security Has Come to Stay

Michelle Ribeiro

After twenty years in the InfoSec industry, my technical debt was becoming too great to avoid, and I decided to understand what all the buzz was about DevOps. Three months later, I was in Ghent, celebrating the tenth anniversary[1] of the movement and meeting figures such as Patrick Debois and Andrew Shafer,[2] the masterminds behind the DevOps idea.

Debois patiently talked about continuous security and how our focus must be to contribute value to the business, to make it resilient, shifting from a reactive security mindset to a proactive approach. On the flight back, I read again *The Phoenix Project*,[3] now giving special attention to the John Pesche character. He was the typical CISO from the waterfall times: a gatekeeper, acting upon fear, in the final stages of development, just before deployment into production. Or before an audit.

I realized that, just like in the book, even after the adoption of DevOps, scheduled security audits remained a reality. Security checks happened when the code was fully baked, against some predefined list of requirements. Weeks later, the audit team would issue a PDF report with hundreds of pages. C-level executives would read only the executive summary and the conclusion. The findings would take another pair of weeks to land in the backlog.

---

1 DevOpsDays 2019 Program (*https://oreil.ly/0WpjW*).

2 Fredric Paul, "The Incredible True Story of How DevOps Got Its Name," New Relic (*https://oreil.ly/XANIc*).

3 Gene Kim, Kevin Behr, and George Spafford, *The Phoenix Project*, 5th Anniversary Edition (*https://oreil.ly/Z0BWe*).

It's easy to see how InfoSec is not adding value to the company's goals. Instead, we are making it lose money. By not separating the secure code from the unapproved code, we delay the release of new features or, even worse, make inevitable the release of insecure applications into the wilds of cyberspace. Add here the surge of cloud-native applications and automated threads and you have the "Adapt or Die" moment for InfoSec.

To adapt, according to the DevSecOps Manifesto,[4] we need to operate like developers and make security and compliance available as code. It must be easily and quickly consumable to foster innovation. In other words, security must become integrated into continuous integration and continuous delivery (CI/CD) software pipelines, decentralizing and automating vulnerability assessments such as secure and dynamic application security tests (SASTs and DASTs).

InfoSec must empower Dev and Ops teams to rapidly fix their code from the earliest possible point in the development process. This is exactly the notion behind the Shift Left concept. Or as John Willis says: "You build it, you secure it."

The hardest part for me was that the average software stack has gotten way too complex and distributed to comprehend. As usual, in-depth security modelling can make complicated things simpler. There are four layers in cloud-native security,[5] the 4 Cs:

1. Code security
2. Container security
3. Cluster security
4. Cloud security

If you are an experienced host security professional, container security will be an easy skill to learn. You can start at the Docker documentation center. Cluster security is a little bit trickier, and the number of container orchestrator alternatives to Kubernetes is growing faster. All you have to do is to start from the basics: learn Kubernetes and expand from there. Grab yourself a copy of *Kubernetes Security*,[6] a book by Liz Rice and Michael Hausenblas.

---

4 DevSecOps (*https://www.devsecops.org*).

5 "Overview of Cloud Native Security," Kubernetes documentation (*https://oreil.ly/aUTbJ*).

6 Liz Rice and Michael Hausenblas, *Kubernetes Security* (O'Reilly, 2018) (*https://oreil.ly/i5WgK*).

Next, cluster security. Read your cloud provider security documentation. Check what tools they recommend. And when you are feeling confident, get ready to introduce Security Chaos Engineering[7] practices to test resilience.

Finally, a word about metrics: one of the pillars of a DevSecOps initiative is measuring security and using it to guide your continuous security strategy. As Dan Geer says, our goal is "to move from a culture of fear to a culture of awareness and then to a culture of measurement."[8]

---

7 Aaron Rinehart and Kelly Shortridge, *Security Chaos Engineering* (O'Reilly, 2020) (*https://oreil.ly/eUYmT*).

8 Dan Geer, "Measuring Security" (*https://oreil.ly/KJjof*).

Cloud Security: A 5,000 Mile View from the Top

Michelle Taggart

Operational cloud technology and services provide tremendous benefits for various businesses, including risk transference. However, moving to a cloud infrastructure without visibility on the service provider's security posture and program puts cloud customers in an unknown vulnerable state.

Operational changes should be symbiotic with security changes. System changes should activate the risk identification review that will update all succeeding processes that depend on the evaluation results. Because business information can present itself in different forms and locations, information management is crucial in enforcing adequate data security and control. Moreover, information may exist in an unstructured format where the misconception that such data is not considered sensitive might be overlooked. Employing a data inventory service powered by AI can help identify information that would generally have been overlooked.

A legally binding agreement through the cloud security agreement, or CSA, between the cloud customer and their cloud security provider, or CSP, provides assurance that a mutual understanding has taken place before doing business. As the CSP customers, in general, relinquish their control over the environment that the CSP manages, the CSA becomes their compensating control over the data that is being processed externally.

As with any other emerging cloud services, cloud-based security offerings also have grown. Businesses have an advantage in having various choices over what security services they can avail to protect their cloud-based data and processes. Procurement, working with IT security, must exercise caution to prevent oversubscription in overlapping security capabilities.

Access management to standard software as a service (SaaS), services should be managed and controlled by employing a cloud access security broker, or CASB, solution. A CASB provides visibility into SaaS services through shadow IT reporting that may not have been previously identified. In addition, the implementation of granular access control to a SaaS that does not offer that level of specificity natively grants additional operations benefit. Not only does a CASB provide security, but it also allows business units functionality where the business did not previously accept the risk of specific accesses.

Because infrastructure has converted to a codebase format, the risk of misconfiguration has vastly increased. As such, businesses should use a cloud security posture management solution, or CSPM, that enforces both an acceptable compliance status and a persistently secure baseline configuration on cloud resources. A common CSPM solution provides continuous monitoring and resource template scanning to address any configuration issues before resource instantiation. Common CSPM solutions can further provide the additional ability to perform automated or scripted remediation for businesses with lean support staff.

Cloud-based automation brings faster time-to-market delivery. However, if security is not involved in the process, the infrastructure could suffer from continuous rebuild to address open vulnerabilities. Adopting a DevSecOps methodology addresses the concern of insecure code while reducing the time it takes to handle such findings after the fact. This process requires a shift in development practice and dealing with the necessary staffing changes and learning curve.

Lastly, businesses must consider cybersecurity insurance to address any residual risk that security controls have not addressed. Because risks are never fully mitigated, cyber insurance provides additional protection for the business if a breach happens.

Balancing the Risk and Productivity of Browser Extensions

Mike Mackintosh

With application accessibility steadily shifting from native desktop applications to the web and the rise of software as a service (SaaS), companies began to see an increase in productivity. This "access anywhere" model removes the need for heavy desktop applications to be installed locally and instead allows visitors to access the data they needed from lightweight web browsers. This approach to application development allows teams to focus on a single, streamlined product offering via the web, which usually correlates to quicker release cycles and improved feature deployment.

Browser extensions are most commonly created by developers to extend the intended functionality of a visited web page. For example, if a web browser has a search box, one extension might extend this element to an omnisearch, allowing the search box to be queried from the URL bar. Alternatively, another extension might replace all the images on a web page with your favorite celebrity. Some of the more productivity-focused extensions have a tendency to take information from an external API and display it inline with the rest of the web page contents, allowing you to view data in a more convenient manner. There has even been a trend for extensions to take advantage of reading all the contents of text boxes, formatting it and checking for grammatical errors, which would then replace the original user input.

These productivity boosters help everyone from project managers to sales teams, developers and analysts alike. However, everything viewed on the web page is accessible to the extension. Web pages are rendered by the browser and generate the viewable web page using a combination of CSS, HTML, and JavaScript. Extensions are usually executed by the browser following the rendering of the page. This allows the extension to read HTML meta tags, which include page titles and cookies, and even make requests on the user's behalf without blocking the user interface from functioning.

Within the source of the web page, especially the title meta tags, companies often reference names of important initiatives, milestones, projects, and clients. Applications like JIRA, Redmine, Trello, Asana, and others will often provide the task or issue name within the title of the page, making it easy for the extension to access it. Web analytic companies often pay extension developers to include tracking mechanisms to gather this information, which more times than not ends up either for sale through their platforms or leaked through a compromise of their own. This could eventually escalate to competitive advantages, resulting in losses to your company. It should come as no surprise why extensions want you to install them. Often it's not because of the productivity boost they provide, but because the data they collect from you is valuable.

There are a few ways you can protect yourself and your organization from malicious browser extensions. Start with limiting their installation if you have the technical capabilities. Perform audits around which extensions are currently installed on corporate devices and what permissions have been granted. It's also a good idea to review the extension source code to see if it's dynamically loading any external web resources that could have access to the referring web page. Lastly, educate your users to not install random extensions, and reinforce what a safe extension might look like.

A safe extension would not execute on every web page, rather only the web page it's intended for. An even safer extension would not request access to cookies, log your user data, or have the ability to make an outbound web request.

Technical Project Ideas Towards Learning Web Application Security

Ming Chow

Quite often, I am asked about technical cybersecurity project ideas from people who want to get into the field. Looking back at my career, the knowledge gained from doing these projects helped me immensely. Each of these projects has an underlying big idea that will prove to be very valuable for the long term. Each of these projects can start out very small and can morph into something big. These projects do not have a significant financial cost, all under $50.00. The only requirement is to have access to a computer of some sort.

Build a Static Website Using HTML, CSS, JavaScript, and Amazon S3

Without using a frontend framework such as Bootstrap, write a simple static website using HTML, CSS, JavaScript, and Amazon S3. One idea for a website is a personal website. I do not recommend using a frontend framework for this project because it provides so much for you where you don't need to understand how things really work. Build the website using a good code editor (e.g., Atom, Sublime, Visual Studio Code).

If your goal is to do web application security, it is necessary to know how the web works. This includes the syntax and structure of HTML, CSS, and JavaScript files. I also included Amazon S3 in this project, not because it is part of AWS, but because of the rash of security incidents involving open S3 buckets exposing troves of secrets. Hence, this is a system that security practitioners should know about.

Create a Blog Using WordPress

Create a blog using WordPress through either its cloud hosting service or by installing it on your web server using the source code. Customize your blog using a theme and install plug-ins.

WordPress powers over 20% of the world's websites. However, WordPress and plug-ins are riddled with vulnerabilities. A serious vulnerability in WordPress or in a popular WordPress plug-in can affect 100,000+ websites. Generally speaking, all WordPress websites follow the same structure. It is beneficial to know the structure of a WordPress website, including where plug-ins, themes, and uploads are stored (in wp-content), and how to administer a WordPress blog (via wp-admin).

Build a Blog App Using a Web Application Framework

Using a web application framework like Django (Python), Ruby on Rails (Ruby), Flask (Python), or Express (Node.js), build a blog app. The official Ruby on Rails tutorial is building a blog app.

A web application framework allows developers to write software with less code. That is, some common tasks can be done with as little as one line— which is both a good and a bad thing. Less code means faster development at the cost of abstracting away how things work. Building a web application will also help you see the many different components (i.e., distributed system) required, including a database and middleware. Using a web application framework also makes it easy for developers to include third-party libraries via a programming language's package manager (e.g., gem for Ruby, pip for Python, npm for Node). The latest OWASP Top 10 now lists "Using Components with Known Vulnerabilities."

The Point of These Projects

Each of the project ideas started with the word "build," "create," or "write." Not a single project mentioned penetration testing, using a security tool, ethical hacking, OSINT, or social engineering. Understanding how things work underneath the hood goes a very long way—the core of security. Once you know the fundamentals and how systems work, you will have a much better sense of what's going on when you use security tools like Metasploit, wpscan, Burp Suite, THC Hydra, Nmap, and countless others.

Monitoring: You Can't Defend Against What You Don't See

Mitch B. Parker

When we think of ransomware and targeted attacks, the approach that has been commonly taken has been to focus on the initial infection vectors. This means checking for phishing emails, breached accounts, or vulnerabilities on exposed systems that connect to internal systems. We do not assume that they're already in the network and moving around laterally to discover what exists without the use of malware. Many of the targeted attacks on health systems have leveraged this approach for maximum effectiveness and have made significant money for the ransomware gangs that employ it. With the lack of two-factor authentication in active enforced usage, security of partner systems, and the number of breached accounts and passwords on the internet, *we need to assume breach and operate as if the adversaries are already present.*

With financial systems, we must monitor them to ensure that people are not using their accounts to engage in improper behavior such as collusion. We also need to monitor them so that we can ensure that the proper controls are in place to protect financial systems integrity to American Institute of Certified Public Accountants (AICPA) standards. This is critical to provide assurances that the company has processes to look for and correct improper behavior, and that there is evidence that the accounting records have not been tampered with.

How do we effectively do this? For security, we need to log all activity on devices and cloud services we control to a security information and event management (SIEM) solution, a service such as Splunk, or a managed security services provider (MSSP). We then need to determine what outlier conditions outside of normal behavior are so we can examine the data for them. In the case of financial systems, it is the controls for separation of duties, collusion, and improper access. Depending on the implementation of the financial system used, the number of controls and processes can vary. We recommend that you engage the services of a licensed public accounting firm to address your organization's specific needs for financial systems.

For detecting improper and potentially malicious computer activity, we need to examine behaviors based on accounts and assigned roles. If an account logs in from an unusual location, such as countries that normally do not conduct business or log in, from a VPN, or from an exit node of a routing network meant to obfuscate, that needs to be flagged and examined. If the account has been logging in to numerous computing resources outside of normal behavior, that also needs to be examined. If the account was dormant for over a month and is suddenly active again, that must be looked at. If there have been accounts created or group memberships changed to include new accounts or new instances with administrator access, that is cause for immediate concern. If there are egress connections from servers that normally do not make outside connections, or significant traffic being exfiltrated from a workstation, this is immediately reason to look at the network for potential compromises.

With logging, correlation, and analysis, behavior that was not immediately obvious comes to the surface. You need to have team members looking at these logs, examining outliers, and addressing issues. Resource allocation to examine and address them for both financial and security systems is paramount. We need to make sure that we promptly investigate and address concerns. We cannot just check the front door. We must assume that those who wish to do us harm are already in our networks and examine activity to protect our financial systems and the networks themselves.

Documentation Matters

Najla Lindsay

In the age of social media and its influence, the one thing that I believe and have learned while on this information security journey is that *documentation* matters. I knew it did from my forensics background, but it really came into play when I decided to start sharing my journey. I highly recommend that you *share your progress*, the good, the bad, and the ugly. Sharing can be via a professional site such as LinkedIn, a social site such as Twitter, or a personal website and/or blog. You may think that what you have said and done has already been published. Truth is, it has, but that is not the point. Your perspective and thought processes matter and the more you share what you know, the more you grow your network and gain valuable insight because people in the community will freely share resources with you.

I cannot stress this enough. The more you share, the more you gain. I have personally used Twitter to document and share my progress and I have learned so much during my journey. I have learned that if you do not ask, the answer will always be *no*. Ask, and ask some more. The more you ask, the more information you obtain, and the more you can decipher for yourself what is the best decision for *you*. Do not focus on it being perfect because it will never be the right time, but I promise you the positives of sharing your progress and asking for clarity in this field will be invaluable to your career progression.

This is your *documentation* of "How It Started versus How It's Going." Documentation will save your life, and the first way to get used to documenting in information security is to start with sharing your progress.

We all have "The Sauce" and there is always a secret ingredient in the sauce. The secret ingredient in the sauce is *you*; your work is the sauce, and that is *your power. You* are *you* and no one can take that away from you, and *you* are your best advocate. *Document* and *share your progress*. For yourself. For those behind you. For the information security community.

The Dirty Truth Behind Breaking into Cybersecurity

Naomi Buckwalter

We are understaffed, overworked, and stressed in cybersecurity.

If you've ever spent any amount of time in cybersecurity, whether it's two weeks or two decades, you probably understand that statement to be true. In a 2019 survey by Nominet, 91% of CISOs say they suffer from moderate or high stress, and 65% of SOC professionals say stress has caused them to think about quitting.[1]

But why are we stressed? It's quite simple. We have too much to do and not enough people to do it.

Not only that, but it is due to this shortage that we are also at an increased risk of data breaches and cybercrime. According to a 2018 study by (ISC)², over 60% of global organizations said they are at moderate or extreme risk of cyberattack due to this shortage.[2] And according to a 2019 report by the IC3 and the FBI, over 1,300 cybercrimes were reported *every day*. US businesses lost a total of 3.5 billion dollars that year alone.[3]

The cybersecurity talent pipeline—the source of incoming entry-level cybersecurity professionals—is unsustainably small. Many cybersecurity hopefuls looking to start a career in cybersecurity are being turned away at the door for not having enough experience. Indeed, the average "entry-level" job in cybersecurity requires five years of experience, a CISSP, and a college degree.

---

1 Simon Whitburn, "CISOs: Life Inside the Perimeter," Nominet, August 27, 2019 (*https://oreil.ly/usEVb*).

2 "Cybersecurity Skills Shortage Soars, Nearing 3 Million," (ISC)² Blog, October 18, 2018 (*https://oreil.ly/u2AMY*).

3 *2019 Internet Crime Report*, IC3 (*https://oreil.ly/a6NfM*).

This doesn't make any sense. There is plenty of entry-level work in cybersecurity. Think about it: asset management, data classification, basic IT security operations, identity and access management—you don't need five years of experience, a CISSP, and a college degree to do these, or pretty much anything, in cybersecurity.

And here's where we need to start admitting to ourselves the dirty truth. We security leaders and veteran cybersecurity professionals are the reason why there are unfilled positions, high turnover, and stress. We are the reason why there are breaches, and if we're honest with ourselves, we're the reason why these same types of breaches will continue to occur well after we retire.

And why is that? It's because we act as *gatekeepers* for cybersecurity. We are afraid of letting people in who don't have the right years of experience, the right number of certifications, or the right college degree. We are doing this to ourselves. We are the reason why new folks are struggling to break into cybersecurity.

Here's what we need to do as a community. We need to break down the gates. We need to let people in. We need to take them as they are, hungry, talented, and eager to learn. We need to stop writing job descriptions for entry-level cybersecurity jobs that require five years of experience in cybersecurity. We need to *teach* them and *mentor* them, and show them the way to what good cybersecurity looks like. We need to train up the next generation of cybersecurity professionals.

I know it's hard to admit, but once you start realizing that we're only hurting ourselves by acting as gatekeepers for people trying to break into cybersecurity, you'll realize that letting people in and giving people a chance is in the best interest of everyone. Cybersecurity is everyone's responsibility. And I hope you remember that the next time you have an opening on your team, or someone reaches out for help. I hope you give someone a chance. Because someone gave me a chance, all those years ago, and I'm willing to bet someone took a chance on you too.

Cloud Security

Nathan Chung

The more things change, the more they stay the same. In the 1960s and 1970s, computing models used mainframes where computing power was centralized. In the 1980s and 1990s, the world shifted to client servers that use the distributed computing model. Now cloud computing is the new normal. Some people call mainframes the cloud before the cloud. It is now essential for cybersecurity professionals to know how to attack and defend the cloud since it is a key skill.

When Amazon introduced Amazon Web Services (AWS) in 2006, cloud computing went mainstream. AWS quickly became the top cloud computing provider in the world with Microsoft and Google introducing cloud services a few years after. Common cloud models include software as a service (SaaS), platform as a service (PaaS), and infrastructure as a service (IaaS). By moving computing resources to a cloud provider, significant amounts of money, energy, and resources are saved while allowing computing resources to be scalable as well as available on demand; this is known as elasticity. In 2020, at the height of the COVID-19 pandemic, the global workforce shifted to remote work, accelerating migrations to the cloud. It is often assumed that cloud computing resources are more resilient to cyberattacks, but that is unfortunately not true.

Cloud resources, especially in public clouds, are hosted on the internet. This increased accessibility makes them vulnerable to common web vulnerabilities and attacks such as denial of service (DoS) and man-in-the-middle (MITM) attacks. The same tools used to detect vulnerabilities and launch attacks against websites are often used against cloud providers. These include Shodan, Burp Suite, and custom tools.

In addition, cloud computing resources are also vulnerable to common traditional cyber threats such as authentication weaknesses, insider threats, and malware. In addition, servers hosted in the cloud still run common operating systems such as Windows and Linux. If they are not patched, they are just as vulnerable as servers that are not hosted in the cloud.

The root cause of most public cyber incidents in cloud environments has been misconfiguration. Similar to early versions of Windows Server, security is not enabled by default, storage is not always encrypted, access permissions tend to not follow least privilege, and network security rules do not restrict traffic. AWS has S3 buckets, Microsoft Azure has blobs, Google Cloud Platform (GCP) has buckets, and open source has Kubernetes. With the increased use of scripting to easily build and manage cloud environments, misconfigurations are even easier and more common than ever.

Similar to offensive strategies, defensive strategies in the cloud use similar methods as traditional on-premises. These include enabling logs to detect cyberattacks, patching, updating antivirus, applying security hardening to reduce the attack surface, network segmentation, and applying defense in depth to have multiple layers of defenses. The need for security increases the demand for cloud security engineers and architects, but unfortunately most cybersecurity professionals are new to the cloud and thus do not have the skills to defend it. The good news is that there are resources and tools you can leverage to learn that are free and easy to learn.

Cloud computing is here to stay. As such, it is critical for cybersecurity professionals to learn how to protect and defend against the cloud. It is now a critical skill for all cybersecurity professionals to learn. Where to start? Entry-level training and certifications such as Cloud+ and Certificate of Cloud Security Knowledge (CCSK) are great places to start. Certified Cloud Security Professional (CCSP) is a mid-level certification. Then there is a focus on specific cloud platforms such as AWS, GCP, or Azure. Each platform has their own training and certifications. The expert-level certifications have specializations such as cloud architects, security engineers, and DevOps engineers. There are also cloud security frameworks that can help. One is NIST 500-292, Cloud Computing Reference Architecture, and the other is the Cloud Security Alliance Cloud Controls Matrix (CCM). These will demonstrate elite skills and capabilities to build and protect cloud environments.

Empathy and Change

Nick Gordon

How do we deal as individuals with change that occurs in both our profession and our companies? What if your company is rapidly hiring and you no longer can tap the relevant person on the shoulder because you no longer know who they are?

Bringing Change

As someone who works in security, you are often the harbinger of change and bad news—we are in charge of looking after the interests of the larger group of the company. You will need to build partnerships across your organization to enact sustainable change. Patching a specific issue will not help when future bugs are introduced—unless you build out the relationships with other teams that can identify and notify you.

This means people skills need to be part of your toolkit, and to complement them you will need a lot of empathy for both those who came before and those you are now working with. Very rarely are people deliberately acting maliciously, and what may look like a poor decision now was often based on the knowledge and tools available at the time.

Mandates Only Work When Someone Is Watching

Sometimes you will need to absolutely mandate a change, but that will have consequences unless you keep it narrow and have already built the relationships. People who were affected will not forget that they did not have a choice.

The long tail also comes up here—anything that was not explicitly covered by the mandate and is either new or otherwise an edge case may not be raised. You will need to be very active to sustain the visibility you have (and you do have visibility into how successful the policy change was, right?).

Write It Down

Anytime something happens, make sure that you write it down. Changes are within the context of a set of options at a given point in time, and future iterations of your team may need to revisit this context. Often with implementations or policies, we have a record of "the what" that can be discovered, but the WHY is also important as a team/company/industry evolves. What was a good decision today may be no longer relevant as technology, people, or the company evolve.

A bonus effect of this is that it increases clarity for both your team and your customers. The act of writing choices explicitly means that the author also has to have a (better) understanding of the choices they are making, and creates an avenue for discussion around less obvious points.

Information Security Ever After

Nicole Dorsett

To anyone determined to succeed in information security, it is a career path that will quickly reveal one truth: to whom much is given, much will be required. If you find yourself fancying the field of InfoSec, rest assured you have made a powerful choice for your future and career. Wherever you are on your journey, there are valuable skills you can begin developing or strengthening that will help you build a positive reputation and strong work ethic to better serve you and your colleagues. It is here that a passion for learning, problem solving, and teamwork can be your recipe for success.

We are fortunate to work in a sector that is coming to embrace diversity and equity. Today, all of us can appreciate major strides in IT by women and minorities, and we all bring diverse backgrounds, talents, and perspectives to the table. Previously, I worked in various administrative and clerical roles in industries ranging from retail, entertainment, and media to insurance, legal, and finance, and every role contributed something to my endeavors in InfoSec.

Whether I was providing customer service, meeting strict deadlines, thriving under pressure, paying attention to details, collaborating with teammates, or being proactive, they were all skill sets I applied to my InfoSec pathway. Still, this path was uncharted territory for me, and there's no denying that it was both exciting and scary. Well, fear not.

The biggest hurdle I overcame at the beginning of this journey was the fear of not being good enough or being in over my head. Once I decided on information security and I knew I enjoyed it, I countered self-defeating thoughts by learning as much as I could, from as many resources possible. I chucked the introvert in me and contacted friends and family working in information security or IT and shared my ambitions while asking for guidance. I networked with individuals and groups through LinkedIn, kept in touch with professors, and later became like a sponge when working among proven leaders in my first IT role as an information security analyst.

It was in this role that I quickly learned what "imposter syndrome" was. I often felt like I didn't know enough or my cover would soon be blown. That nonsense didn't sit well with me. So, I started listening to podcasts, reading InfoSec magazines and blogs, and investing time in earning certifications. Increasing my knowledge base simultaneously boosted my confidence.

In all of your getting, get understanding. I wasn't shy about asking questions when I needed clarity or wanted to understand the bigger picture. Sure enough, understanding processes and the inner workings of the teams I supported further helped me perform and enjoy my job. Whether you are upholding the golden rule that directs us to understand the assets we are protecting and where they are (logically or physically), or you're simply troubleshooting systems, do it in a way that exhibits care and commitment. Yet never forget to take care of yourself.

Allow for the development and sacrifice your career deserves, but let your values and self-worth be your compass. As you yield the fruits of your labor, enjoy them. Ensure your team's needs are met while also acknowledging your own. Indulge in much needed breaks, spend quality time with loved ones, and determine what balance looks like for you. The possibilities are endless when it comes to blazing a trail in InfoSec, so remain positive, prepared, and vigilant. Finally, always give as much as you hope to gain, and you too can live information security ever after.

Don't Check It In!

Patrick Schiess

During high school, my friends and I spent countless hours trying to hack each other. One day, I stumbled upon an easy way to trick them into inadvertently exposing their passwords through administrative error logs. Using an early 2000s popular online bulletin board software as a medium, I lured my friends into what I assured them would be an engaging space to share thoughts on topics such as video games, programming, and music. I explained that all they had to do was log in to the website using their regular credentials and they would be good to go. However, when they attempted to do so, the software gave an error: `Invalid password : [P@55w0rd!]`, which ultimately ended up in the error logs. As an administrator, I was able to view the logs to find their passwords and subsequently hijack their emails, gamer accounts, and web hosts—ultimately winning our juvenile "capture the flag" competition.

Today, the internet is a very different place. Secure coding practices and multifactor authentication provide enhanced protection against these types of rudimentary password attacks. As security constraints have evolved, social engineering and phishing may seem easily avoidable for *user* accounts. However, *application* passwords and secrets may still be at risk of getting compromised unless the proper precautions are taken.

At a former employer, enterprise development teams shared a single communal source code management platform. As licensed users of the platform, developers had the ability to (at minimum) view the source code as well as any changes, history, etc., for the entire organization. One day, while reviewing the change history for an application's code repository, I discovered a historical commit from a couple of years prior. Much to my surprise, the commit included a configuration file with an application administrative service account password stored in cleartext! On the subsequent commit, the password was removed by the developer and replaced with a reference to a secrets vault. I decided to check and see if the password was still valid, and sure enough, I was able to log in using the administrative credentials.

Although this developer caught their mistake more or less immediately and removed the application password from the source code, it was etched into the commit history for anyone in the future to stumble upon. Unfortunately, the only way to rectify this mistake was to delete the entire code repository, reupload the code, and recycle the application password. Luckily for my company, I had good intentions and did not use the privileged account access for evil.

Application secrets and passwords can be at risk if left unchecked. It is important to make sure that secrets are never stored in cleartext in configuration files, checked in to source code repositories, or (as in my high school hacking escapades) exposed through administrative error logs. It is also a good idea to cycle application passwords regularly, if for no other reason than to cover your tail if you are the developer who accidentally commits it to the source code server.

Threat Modeling for SIEM Alerts

Phil Swaim

As security professionals in a security operations center (SOC), there are a great range of alerts that will be available to you. Antivirus, firewalls, intrusion detection and prevention systems (IDS/IPS), identity and access management (IAM), data loss prevention (DLP), and many other tools and systems will generate alerts that may or may not be helpful to your SOC in determining if an adverse event has occurred.

Overlogging and overenabling these alerts could result in high false-positive rates, which end up distracting the SOC from possible real threats in the environment getting through.

So what to do? Threat model your alerts!

Identify a target of interest in your environment you wish to defend from adversaries. Draw it or write its name on the right side of a chart. Leave some room on the right for later. This could be data, a process, or even a person in your organization.

Identify interested adversaries, such as hacktivists, nation states, cybercriminals, or insider threats, and place them on the left of the chart in separate rows. You will find that some adversaries prefer to use different initial vectors.

Identify likely initial vectors and list those by adversary to the right of the adversary list. A targeted phish, an insider using USB, and drive-by malware downloads are some examples.

Identify points of lateral movement from the initial vector towards the target. Privilege escalation, Remote Desktop Protocol (RDP), Secure Shell (SSH) Protocol, or even internal spear-phishing are possible methods of lateral movement. Think about what is most likely or even easy to accomplish in your environment given an initial vector. This is where the model expands quite a bit. The lateral movement steps should end at the target. Focus on the shortest paths to the target from the initial vectors.

Identify next moves after the target is acquired and place them to the right of the target. This should show how the adversary will use their access to the target, e.g., data tampering/theft, ransomware, selling access, or even submitting fraudulent jobs through a business process.

Identify points of visibility along the attack path model and draw vertical lines through or between each step of the attack path, including tools for email security, endpoint security, netflows, firewalls, IDS signatures, database access logs, FTP logs, or anything that would have visibility to shed light on what an adversary might be up to. These points of visibility now can feed an alert or series of alerts tailored specifically to the model you just crafted!

Paying special attention to the logs associated with the model, you can write out the logic for your security information and event management (SIEM) engineers to build an alert with. You might have to build multiple alerts if different adversaries take different paths.

Playbooking responses to the alert is important as well. Be sure to include a chart of the model as well as a synopsis to help readers understand the context expected for the alert.

Annually, your team should review each alert and determine if their threat models are valid. Do the models need adjustment? Do you have the needed logs from various sources? Have there been changes to log sources available? Is the playbook still relevant to the model? Is the false positive rate acceptable? The important thing to remember when threat modeling is that in reality, all things are possible, but you should try to keep your models simple and based on what is most likely to happen in your organization. Align with your architecture program to help them understand where preventative/detective control gaps are. Once you have threat modeled alerts in place, you will have better confidence in your SOC's ability to respond to threats to your organization. You can also present more contextual metrics to the board and leadership.

Security Incident Response and Career Longevity

Priscilla Li

A Security Incident Response Team (SIRT) plays a critical role in a company. This is a team of professionals responsible for preventing, detecting, and responding to security incidents. Most incident response teams are made up of the following roles:

Triage analyst
> Evaluate incoming alerts, identify suspicious activities, and determine a disposition for each alert. Identify areas of opportunity for areas of automated response.

Detection engineer
> Build and write detection alerts relevant to your environment. Perform threat hunting with the telemetry available in your environment. Respond to high-priority security incidents.

With increasing security threats and breaches, a SIRT has a major responsibility when a security incident happens. Incident responders often have to work under pressure to assess and respond to threats through intrusion detection, security auditing, and risk analysis. In order to experience career longevity in this line of work, here are three tips on how to combat burnout:

Teamwork
> Recognize that managing security incidents is TEAMwork. The responsibility does not fall solely on the incident responder or manager. Incident response teams are critical. These teams typically include an Incident Commander, a Lead Incident Responder, and a Communication Lead. The role of the Incident Responder focuses on collecting and analyzing all evidence to help determine the root cause and impact. They

are then able to direct other security analysts in log reviews for a potential compromise.

Decompress and reconnect

Managing and handling security incidents is draining mentally, physically, and emotionally. When stress and expectations pile up during an incident, it is easy for one to feel overwhelmed and burnt out—especially when the incidents can go on for hours or days. Request backup support if you need a break from the intense situation. Go for a quick breather and clear your mind. This decompression time will help to bring some clarity as well as a new perspective on the incident. Once you are ready, reconnect back and you will find yourself in a better position to manage and handle the incident again.

Post-incident evaluation

Every incident is a learning opportunity. After the security incident, there is time for reflection and evaluating room for improvement that can tighten up the security posture in your environment. Do not look at it as a defeat but rather a lesson learned to improve and build greater detection and automation. After all the chaos and intensity of the incident, the postmortem kickoff will be the time to review what went well, what didn't, and what to improve on. Some examples are:

- Evaluate the changes made in your environment during the incident, such as the creation of an ad hoc alert, security changes to systems, etc.

- Identify additional tools or resources that will improve the team's incident response and detection posture, including areas where automation can be built by the team to speed up time to remediate.

After reflecting on an incident, you will be in a much better position to prevent similar incidents and on your way to building a more secure environment.

Remember, incident response is a marathon, not a sprint!

Incident Management

Quiessence Phillips

I've spent most of my career in incident response and the larger threat management discipline—forming, merging, and maturing programs. Threat management can be considered the hub of the cybersecurity organization, because whether you're preparing for, understanding, or responding to threats, the vantage point of the group allows for it to inform and be informed by all other areas of cybersecurity. As we all know, threats will always exist, but how we manage them is crucial to effectively de-risking the business. The standards for an incident response capability are widely known —see the NIST *Computer Security Incident Handling Guide* (*https://oreil.ly/ Qf0B5*); however, the way in which these standards are developed, executed, and evolved vary by organization. Incident response is a discipline that is largely qualifiable and not always quantifiable. Using the known phases of incident response—preparation, detection, analysis, containment, eradication, recovery, and post-incident activity—incident responders should ask themselves, can I quantify the end of each phase?

When you are waist deep in an incident response engagement, the last thing you want to hear is, "When will this incident be contained?" But the question is inevitable, as a host of parties (communications/media relations, general counsel, human resources, impacted business executives, etc.) require this insight to help inform decision making.

So, how do you get in front of the inquiries? My answer to that is simple: frameworks. Methodologies and frameworks are a staple for incident response, as they help expedite response activities and build a defensible case. If you build a strong framework for how you conduct incident response, socialize the framework, and make your activities visible, you reduce friction for your responders. For example, using the containment phase, containment strategies should be developed for various types of incidents, the strategies should be socialized with all parties that may be involved, and progress on execution of the strategy should be made visible to appropriate parties. Development of containment strategies allows teams to consider and test all tasks involved, ensures integrations with other groups are fluid, and provides insight into the work that will be performed by incident responders.

Once the containment strategies are developed and socialized, the containment calculation comes into play—this is a formal and quantifiable method of calculating the end of the containment phase. For example, if your group has standardized the usage of the Mitre ATT&CK® framework (*https://attack.mitre.org*) throughout your detection and response program, the techniques should be well known to your executives. The high-level techniques can be aligned to a score based on tasks associated with incident response activities related to containment (i.e., quarantine host, reset credentials). Based on the aforementioned containment strategies, a framework can be developed that assigns a score to each task along with a threshold score for when containment has been reached. This helps quantify phases of the incident response life cycle and removes the current and often ambiguous nature of making these determinations.

"But what about the visualization?" you say. As part of your incident response process, someone or a host of people should be tracking every action taken, who performed the action, when, and why. Depending on your organization and what is important to your executives, you can determine how to properly categorize the information to make it easily consumable. Perhaps your executives want to know who is working on incident response, what evidence has been collected, what percentage of tasks are completed, what phase you are in, etc. With that inner knowledge, you can use a visualization program that takes static data and publishes it to a dashboard for your executives. I'm sure you can imagine the reduction in questions and/or interruptions you'll experience as a result of this.

Structure over Chaos

Rob Newby

The security industry, particularly when starting out in it, can seem like a mass of technology and/or processes with no real thread. Or a mass of people with no direction. And often it *is* one or more of those things.

It does not help that security originated from the most technical of disciplines, information technology. Indeed, many CISOs still report to CIOs, opinions on which range wildly and always elicit frenzied debate—quite another discussion altogether.

Many who work in IT pride themselves in deep knowledge in a particular area: we all like to visit the expert to get our technology fixed properly the first time and we admire deep knowledge more than we admire general knowledge—it is human nature.

Unfortunately, particularly at organizational scale, that also gives rise to silos in working. Technical specialists can be protective of their knowledge and skills, and while few actively act to block others out, use of terminology, acronyms, and pack behaviors among the elite can inadvertently cause a "them and us" type of culture that works against the business. In business, the generalists who can bring teams together win out, which only goes to further drive a wedge between technicians and business practitioners.

What helps with the orientation of cybersecurity within the business and coordination within cybersecurity departments is structure. But in business, structure is often regarded as being restrictive. Mention the word *governance* and not only will people disengage, but it conjures up voluminous rule books, red tape, and bureaucracy. This does not have to be the case.

Far simpler than complex rule sets is the use of frameworks. I often use the analogy of building a house when describing frameworks, and to distinguish them from control sets. A framework is a blueprint; it tells you what a house looks like. Controls are bricks, they are the things you need to build the house with. Control sets, therefore, are collections of bricks, arranged in the order you need them, or in easily accessible buckets. You need both blueprints and bricks, but without a blueprint you can't show other people what the house should look like, you can't decide where the bricks are going to go, and you don't know where you will end up.

Security strategy is, in fact, relatively easy. Security is *roughly* the same in any environment, a set of processes, and of course, some of them don't apply in some contexts or have more prominence in others. For example, data protection is important where legal influence has primacy and automated incident management comes to the fore in Fintechs, but the processes are basically the same.

All of which brings me to the NIST Cybersecurity Framework. If you don't know it yet, look it up. Very simply it talks about security being a set of functions:

Each of these functions breaks down into categories, and those into subcategories. At the subcategory level instructions are explicit enough to describe a process that contributes to security. However, the framework is not prescriptive or restrictive. Like a blueprint, it is a set of guidelines as to what security should look like, described as end-to-end processes.

Its simplicity is its brilliance. Not only can you see what security looks like immediately, you can describe that to other people, at any level of the business. Inside your own team, you can show reporting lines and ownership of controls and indicate where potential gaps are. Ownership of processes is somewhat of a holy grail in security management—in simple terms, having someone on the hook for an area of security ensures that the area stays looked after. Rather than making everyone read and sign policies and standards, make sure people are engaged with their responsibilities.

CWE Top 25 Most Dangerous Software Weaknesses

Rushi Purohit

Common Weakness Enumeration (CWE™) is a community-developed list of common software and hardware weaknesses that have quality and security ramifications. "Weaknesses" are flaws, faults, bugs, or other errors in software or hardware implementation, code, design, or architecture that if left unaddressed could result in systems, networks, or hardware being vulnerable to attack. CWE serves as a common language, a measuring stick for security tools, and a baseline for weakness identification, mitigation, and prevention efforts.

Targeted at both the development and security practitioner communities, the main goal of CWE is to educate software and hardware architects, designers, programmers, etc., on how to eliminate the most common mistakes as early in the software development life cycle (SDLC) as possible. Ultimately, use of CWE helps prevent the kinds of security vulnerabilities that have plagued the software and hardware industries and place enterprises at risk. This, in return, helps save money in the long run as well as reduce liability that occurs through these flaws.

With over 900 weaknesses in the CWE corpus, the CWE Team helps the community prioritize the list via the annual Top 25 Most Dangerous Software Weaknesses list (CWE Top 25). It is a demonstrative, data-driven list of the most common and impactful issues experienced over the previous two calendar years. These weaknesses are dangerous because they are often easy to find and exploit, allowing adversaries to completely take over a system, steal data, or prevent an application from working. The CWE Top 25 is a valuable community resource that can help developers, testers, static tool analysis vendors, and users—as well as business leaders, project managers, security researchers, and educators—provide insight into the most severe and current security weaknesses.

To create the annual list, the CWE Team leverages publicly available Common Vulnerabilities and Exposures (CVE®) data and related CWE mappings found within the National Vulnerability Database (NVD), as well as the Common Vulnerability Scoring System (CVSS) scores associated with each of the CVEs. A formula is then applied to the data to score each weakness based on prevalence and severity. This approach provides an objective look at what vulnerabilities are currently seen in the real world, creates a foundation of analytical rigor built on publicly reported vulnerabilities instead of subjective surveys and opinions, and makes the process easily repeatable.

The CWE Top 25 list can be summarized by three high-level categories that each contain multiple CWE entries:

Insecure Interaction Between Components
> This refers to insecure ways in which data is sent and received between separate components, modules, programs, processes, threads, or systems. These include CWEs like Cross-Site Scripting, SQL Injection, OS Command Injection, Improper Input Validation, and more.

Risky Resource Management
> This refers to ways in which software does not properly manage the creation, usage, transfer, or destruction of important system resources. These include CWEs like Improper Restriction of Operations Within the Bounds of a Memory Buffer, Uncontrolled Resource Consumption, Improper Limitation of a Pathname to a Restricted Directory (Path Traversal), and more.

Porous Defenses
> These are related to defensive techniques that are often misused, abused, or simply ignored. These include CWEs like Improper Authentication, Use of Hard-Coded Credentials, Incorrect Permission Assignment for Critical Resource, and more.

To view the latest CWE Top 25 list, visit *https://cwe.mitre.org* or type "CWE Top 25" into a search engine.

Threat Hunting Based on Machine Learning

Saju Thomas Paul and
Harshvardhan Parmar

There are different methods used by organizations to increase cybersecurity defenses. One such method is "threat hunting," which provides an opportunity to uncover advanced threats in an environment that are typically not detected with traditional SIEM-based tools. This article focuses on how threat hunting can use analytical models to search *for tactics, techniques, and procedures* (TTPs) within an environment. Typical attacker TTPs are often derived from indicators of compromise (IoCs) like IPs associated with threat actors or malware, compromised domains, and malware signatures and behaviors.

The formal approach presented here describes how we are leveraging the TTPs from the ATT&CK framework (*https://attack.mitre.org*). to ensure high detection rates in hunting with the use of advanced detection models based on machine learning. In this article, we will be covering the approach with the help of a use case that impacts almost all organizations—a *malicious software or PUP* (potentially unwanted program) that gets installed in an organization's environment that is calling home and/or is stealing data.

Case Study

Modus operandi

We observed a malicious extension put up on the Google Play Store to create an illusion of trust, scamming users to download this extension and thus leading to compromise of users' telemetry data and other sensitive details, including credentials. This extension when installed successfully would read sensitive information and connect to the external world for the ultimate goal to exfiltrate data or redirect it to ads/campaigns.

Detection method

The initial trigger was one of the advanced detection models that we have created for Tactic TA0011 (*https://oreil.ly/TA0011*).[1] In this hunting model, we detected an abnormal connection (*Deviated Behavior*) towards an entity (IP) that was performing persistent beaconing activity. Based on this, we invoked our playbook and were able to detect other techniques/tactics of the MITRE framework. During the investigation, we found validation against other tactics (like T1176 (*https://oreil.ly/T1176*), T1503 (*https://oreil.ly/T1503*), and T1185 (*https://oreil.ly/T1185*)) using models like *Process Injection, Suspicious Processes, Privilege Command Execution,* etc., and were able to determine that the activity identified was indeed malicious. Based on the detection, we prevented the attack from moving to the next stage of the threat life cycle, i.e., moving to the tactics of Collection (T1056 (*https://oreil.ly/T1056*)) and Impact (TA0040 (*https://oreil.ly/TA0040*)).

Thus, by correlating the various TTPs that are part of the ATT&CK framework, we were able to successfully detect the attack at an early stage and prevent a potential breach by leveraging the usage of threat hunting machine learning models. Additionally, we were able to identify the rogue app on the Google Play Store in a network.

To conclude, anomaly detection using artificial intelligence and machine learning has been more prominent in the industry to uncover unknown attacks and threats. With such usage of machine learning, it is very evident that newer technologies/products will shift their focus from traditional use case detection to advanced threat hunting models. As products and security tools increase their usage of AI and machine learning models, it is important that security professionals are knowledgeable of different machine learning models and how to use the output to detect anomalous behavior.

---

1 All the tactics can be viewed online (*https://oreil.ly/omgif*).

Get In Where You Fit In

Sallie Newton

First, welcome to the field of cybersecurity. The most important thing you need to know about cybersecurity is that security is not all bits and bytes. You do not need to be able to code or hack into systems to add value to this field. Cybersecurity professionals come from a plethora of disciplines. In fact, I know many InfoSec professionals from what might seem like unrelated backgrounds far removed from tech, like nursing, finance, and fast-food restaurants. What's the relation? HIPAA, FinSAC, and PCI-DSS. My motto is: get in where you fit in!

Personally, I wondered if my business degree would help to prepare me for a career in cybersecurity. As it turns out, my business degree has served me well in this field. Cybersecurity is about risk to the business. Being able to quickly and accurately convey cybersecurity risk factors to management is a much needed skill set.

One such role at the intersection of cybersecurity and business is policy writing. Policy is the foundation of an InfoSec program; without it you have complete anarchy. Understanding the importance of policy is critical to an effective information security program. As a consultant, I worked a lot with policies and procedures and enjoyed helping companies increase their security postures by implementing rules best suited for their environment. Policies and procedures are not a one-size-fits-all endeavor. The reality is that you don't actually see much of the work that goes into policy, procedures, standards, and baselines. There is no fanfare for documentation. Yet, if done well, these documents could make the difference in you not seeing your enterprise on the news or, dare I say, trending on Twitter.

Typically, policies and procedures are driven by compliance requirements like NIST, ISO, and PCI, etc. That said, let me be very clear, you can be in compliance AND insecure. There is an expectation of continuous improvement. I always advise my clients to treat compliance requirements as a baseline; once achieved, move beyond compliance to improve your security posture.

When creating your policies, ensure that your policies make sense for your environment.

In addition to being aligned with your company's mission, ensure your policies align with your current culture, not your aspirational culture. If culture and policy are not in alignment, culture will eat policy for breakfast.

The real trick is finding a way to communicate. Get buy-in and enforce these policies, procedures, baselines, and standards without overwhelming your workforce. Management's understanding, buy-in, and support is critical to the effectiveness and success of an information security program. Oftentimes, a breach is the result of policy violations. Ensure all policies, procedures, standards, and baselines are up to date, published, easily accessible, trained, educated, frequently reminded, and enforced as needed.

Lastly, there seems to be an increase in the sentiment that employees are the weakest link. The reality is a lack of education and focus on employee impact to a security program has created an environment for employees to be identified as a fruitful attack vector. By not prioritizing our employees as key stakeholders in enterprise information security programs, we as security practitioners have placed a target on employees' backs. A bad actor only needs to deceive one untrained employee in order to use their access privileges to not only enter our environments but to exit our environments with valuable data in tow. That said, define your employee training policies and procedures to prioritize the commitment to educate your employees to be fortresses for your enterprises. It is important to empower and respect employees, not blame and shame them.

Look Inside and See What Can Be

Sam Denard

Static analysis is a testing technique that reveals an analysis target's behavior when the expression of that behavior is separated from the analysis by access, location, and/or time.

For example, a testing agent may have source code but no executable; or an executable but no permission to run it; or only requirements documents. Regardless, static analysis applies certain processes and techniques to the available source material.

The purpose of static analysis is to identify and understand an analysis target's possible behaviors. (The existence of behavior is of concern here, not its likelihood of occurrence.) The analysis goal is to improve or otherwise control that behavior.

Source material is anything that expresses, describes, or reflects the analysis target's behavior. This includes software in all its forms (source code, requirements, design documents, test scripts, installation procedures, etc.) as well as higher-level documents (manuals, EULAs, and contracts). The hardware controlled by the software or on which it runs is also included. Software is created and used by humans; consequently, authors' skill and intent as well as user actions, whether benign or malicious, are also considered.

Organizational processes create the management and cultural context for analyses; this includes testing mandates, scope, resource allocation, and analysis recommendation enforcement. Processes may be implemented with policy and training; however, processes are enhanced by analysts' effective communication with decision makers.

The essence of static analysis is the technique employed by analysts. In addition to basic technical skills, consider the following:

Speedy mindful judgment

Analyses are time-limited and may contend with thousands of issues. Careful but speedy judgment without excessive second-guessing is a skill to be cultivated.

Tool mastery and results evaluation/validation

Timely and effective analysis demands use of tools; however, tools are imperfect. Analysts must understand their tools well enough to separate tool-generated artifacts from genuine issues in the analysis target.

Patience and tedium tolerance

Static analysis is important but requires repetitive, long-term attention to fine detail. Frankly, it can be boring. Procedural checklists, periodic breaks, alternating tasks, coworking, or any other technique that maintains analyst focus is recommended.

Technical and context research

Analysis targets will likely have unfamiliar features; an analyst will have to become familiar quickly.

Analysis target industry expertise

Software is written about something real. Understanding more of that reality allows an analyst to better understand the software.

Interaction with and evaluation of people

Sometimes, analysis evidence is not documented; it may have to be extracted from a person. Conversational techniques may make all the difference.

Reporting

Merely discovering issues is not sufficient. Stating them clearly and offering solutions will produce better results.

Teaching and explanation

The only way to ensure long-term software improvement is to help authors improve their skills, or at least their actions. Diplomacy may be required, but perfection is not. Collegial partnerships go a long way towards getting the job done.

Personal responsibility

Financial, schedule, and other project management pressures can be considerable. An analyst may need the strength to stand their technical ground and the wisdom to find common ground.

Continuous skill development

Software developers practice software synthesis; this builds the skills required to analyze software. Static analysts practice software analysis; this does not maintain their synthesis skills. And, eventually, their analysis skills will degrade. Dedicated static analysts must actively work to prevent this degradation.

Static analysis is the oldest of the software testing techniques; long ago, it was a major part of getting a program to work at all. Today, static analysis is still an essential part of any test plan.

DevOps for InfoSec Professionals

Sasha Rosenbaum

The term "DevOps" first appeared in 2009, at the eponymous DevOpsDays conference in Belgium.[1] Since then, the term has become popular in the industry and evolved to cover a range of related concepts. In this article, we will review the two primary pillars of DevOps: culture and automation.

Culture

As computer science matured as a field, IT departments began to split vertically along the technology stack, creating separate teams for development, QA, application security, operations, and so on. In large organizations, these teams were often separated by a ticketing system, with lengthy handoffs and significant administrative overhead.

To make matters worse, it appeared that the teams had opposite incentives—developers were asked to create new features as quickly as possible, whereas operations were asked to prevent system outages. Since most outages occurred during new releases, operations were reluctant to push any changes to production. Many organizations delivered software on a two- to three-year cadence, and the process of creating a production-ready version could take months. Applications were often "down for maintenance" for entire weekends. Speed of innovation appeared to be in conflict with reliability.

As the world moved increasingly towards a software as a service (SaaS) model, organizations needed a way to deliver continuous updates while maintaining 24/7 availability. The idea of DevOps was to break the silos and create cross-functional collaboration within organizations to shorten the software delivery life cycle. DevOps practitioners did not aim to combine specifically development and operations, but rather to make it easier for the

---

1 "DevOps," Wikipedia (*https://oreil.ly/vDJ9w*).

entire IT departments to work towards a common goal—delivering value to users.

It is worth noting that despite the goal to break silos, the new trend created numerous additional job titles, including DevOps, Release, Automation, and Delivery Engineer, designating teams responsible specifically for software delivery life-cycle automation.

Automation

It turns out that software delivery speed is not in conflict with reliability. From the State of DevOps (DORA) reports, *2019 Acceleration State of DevOps Report (https://oreil.ly/2DRxA)*, we know that the organizations that push to production multiple times a day have a much lower change failure rate and take less time to recover from incidents. It becomes clear that pushing to production is like developing a muscle—the more you use it, the stronger it gets.

In terms of automation, DevOps is closely related to CI/CD (continuous integration and continuous delivery)[2]. CI/CD is the approach of producing software in short cycles, and ensuring that it can be reliably released to production at any time, so the decision to trigger a release becomes a business decision, rather than a technical one. The idea is that the entirety of the software delivery life cycle, from ideation to implementation to production operations, should be automated as much as possible.

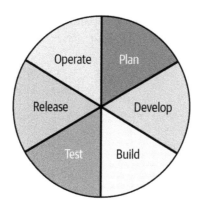

---

2 "Continuous Delivery," Wikipedia (*https://oreil.ly/WK41Y*).

Mature organizations have processes and tools that track and automate software delivery through every stage of the life cycle, with application security ideally being involved in all stages. The CI/CD pipelines often automate the deployment of application infrastructure (typically VMs or container orchestrators such as Kubernetes), building and testing the application code, and releases to different environments such as test, staging, and production.

Mature CI/CD pipelines usually include software composition analysis (SCA) and static and dynamic application security testing (SAST/DAST) tools to facilitate application security testing, and have quality, security, and compliance gates at multiple stages of the delivery process. Life-cycle automation also provides thorough audit trails for the entire change process, helping organizations satisfy compliance requirements.

To summarize, DevOps is about cross-team collaboration and automating the software delivery life cycle to ensure consistent and predictable outcomes.

Recommended Reading

Forsgren, Nicole, Jez Humble, and Gene Kim. *Accelerate: The Science of Lean Software and DevOps: Building and Scaling High Performing Technology Organizations.* Portland, OR: IT Revolution Press, 2018.

Freeman, Emily. *DevOps for Dummies.* Hoboken, NJ: John Wiley & Sons, Inc., 2019.

Kim, Gene, Kevin Behr, and George Spafford. *The Phoenix Project (A Novel About IT, DevOps, and Helping Your Business Win).* Portland, OR: IT Revolution Press, 2018.

Get Familiar with R&R (Risk and Resilience)

Shinesa Cambric

No matter where you are in your career journey, an area that all information security professionals should become familiar with is R&R. I don't mean rest and relaxation (although those are extremely important too). The R&R all security professionals should be aware of is Risk and Resilience. These concepts are foundational to why companies hire security professionals and a key component to why our industry exists. If there isn't a risk to an asset, there isn't a need to secure it. Where risk does exist, processes need to be in place to protect against it. Those protections need to be multilayered and designed in such a way that a business can continue to operate despite exposure to risk. If it can't, it ceases to exist. Risk is such an important area that there are certifications solely dedicated to understanding what risk is, calculating its effects, and determining the most cost-effective solutions for treating it.

For those who are new to information security, understanding which risks you are addressing will provide you with the high-level context for the value of the work you are performing and its importance to your company. We have to remember that security operations exist to support business objectives, and not the other way around. There are several questions you should frequently ask of yourself and those in the security organization when performing a task or implementing a new project or tool. First, what risk is this addressing? Next, why is the risk being addressed this way? When and how would this risk be an issue if it's not addressed this way? Who is being exposed and/or protected from the risk by the security actions I'm performing? And what other alternatives exist for addressing this?

In addition to asking these questions to understand what risks exist within your business, you should also understand how these risks impact business objectives. Seeing the bigger picture of the role of security within an organization will help you to build a strategic mindset as you progress in your career. Take time to periodically assess how the security functions around you support the business in meeting operational objectives. And remember for security operations of a business to really be successful, there should be a clear benefit to how it keeps the business operational (supports business resilience).

For those who are more senior in the information security industry, the concepts of risk and resilience are even more important. I believe within the core of most security professionals is a desire to find and close every loophole an attacker could use, but the reality is we are working with finite resources, along with time and budget constraints. This means business risks have to be known and prioritized so that we address those items that are the greatest risk to business operations and implement solutions that provide the greatest opportunity for resilience. At higher levels of leadership, security is routinely reduced to calculations of cost-benefit analysis. Here it not only helps to understand how to perform these calculations, but to build camaraderie with your business partners in governance, risk, and compliance (GRC). Your partners in the GRC space will not only help you get that bird's-eye view of business risk and where security operations can address risk and resilience, but they can also be your allies in obtaining the budget needed to do so.

Password Management

Siggi Bjarnason

I am a very sharing kind of guy and believe strongly that sharing is caring. I am happy to share absolutely anything and everything, with literally only two exceptions. I am not big on sharing my toothbrush, and I absolutely do not under any circumstances share my passwords. There are two kinds of password sharing that I am totally against. The first is sharing a password between sites. I make sure every site I have an account on has a totally unique password. The second type of sharing I'm against is sharing passwords with anyone else. No one has any of my passwords, not even my spouse. You are probably thinking to yourself, that sounds like a lot of passwords to keep track of, and you would be correct in that thinking. I have several hundred passwords in active use. How do I keep track of all those passwords, you ask? Do I have them all memorized? Absolutely not. I'm lucky if I can remember two passwords. I use a password manager to keep track of my passwords.

A password manager is an application that is specifically designed to track passwords securely. Care needs to be taken when choosing a password manager, to choose one that fits your needs and one that is well respected and well-known to be highly secure. When looking for a password manager, look for the following:

- Strong data encryption, ideally using at least AES 256-bit level of encryption or stronger.
- Multifactor authentication (MFA). The best ones offer multiple options to choose from.
- Is the solution monitored for access, data corruption, and operational issues?
- Can you access the password manager anytime and everywhere you need to?

When you use the same passwords on multiple sites, if one of those sites is compromised, all the sites that use the same password are compromised. This can become a huge headache. While maintaining hundreds of passwords is a bit of a pain, it is nowhere near the pain of having to change passwords across hundreds of sites when one of those sites has a cyber incident. Also, having data from one site in the hands of cybercriminals is bad enough; enabling them to have access to ten sites because they all share the same password is ten times as bad.

Another thing regarding password management that is important is choosing a good password. In the past, there was a lot of talk about the complexity of the password being essential. Passwords needed to have uppercase, lowercase, numbers, and a special character. This ended up with everyone choosing something like Fall2020! as their password. This is a horrible password and can be breached in a fraction of a second. Recent research shows that length is the most important aspect of a password. Don't think of a password as a single word, rather as a phrase that is at least 15 characters long. I try to make all my passwords at least 20 characters long. Many password managers also have a password generator function that will generate just a random string of characters. This is most secure but impossible to remember. For a more memorable phrase, think of a phrase that no one is likely to guess. Avoid site or app names and well-known aspects of you or your life. It does not have to be grammatically correct, or even make sense. Something along the lines of "NittingCowDancesMoon!" would be a good password except for the fact that it is published here as an example. It is both strong because of length and matches complex rules.

Let's Go Phishing

Siggi Bjarnason

The majority of security incidents happen due to phishing, and I have a sure-fire way to avoid becoming a phishing victim. Just don't click on links in emails or open attachments. Yes, I do realize that this advice is about as useful as telling someone to stop smoking or not eat donuts. It is a lot easier said than done. Also, any suggestion that starts with the word "just" tends to be suspect. Hear me out, though, as I explain how this could be implemented.

This needs to start with a culture of not sending unexpected links or attachments around. There needs to be an internal document repository site that is automatically a part of everyone's bookmarks. Rather than attaching a file or sending a link to it, in the email describe where on the internal site it can be found. Something like "the document can be found under documents > ProjectX > design."

This way, people will fall out of the habit of clicking on links or opening attachments, and it will start to become abnormal and strange to do so. Emails offering free ice cream and the like will continue to be tempting because human beings love games and contests. They especially like getting something free. If you set up an internal contest about finding malicious emails and notifying the security team, that could satisfy that urge.

Rather than trying to train folks in deciphering URLs and determining if the link is valid or not, make the training situational:

- They are signing up for a service that requires providing their email address, the sign-up process says a confirmation email is being sent, and you need to click on it to confirm the registration. If you get an email within a few minutes that looks like it is from that organization, then clicking on that link carries a relatively low risk.

- They are on a conference call. Someone on the call says they are sending a document to everyone. They explain what it is all about and why it needs to be sent around rather than posted to the document repository.

When you get an email from that person that matches the description, opening it carries a relatively low risk.

- If they receive an email with a link or attachment that doesn't match either of those scenarios, claiming to be from an internal contact or other known contacts, look up their contact information in the internal company contact list and call them up or send them a chat message asking them what this is about and why they chose to send it in an email rather than post it on the document repository. If they get a satisfactory explanation, the risk of opening it is low. Never reply to the email or use other contact information in the email. If alternative contact information is not available outside of that email, consider the email malicious. If the explanation for the email seems off or sketchy or the sender seems sketchy, the safe move is to consider the email malicious.

Additionally, it would be a good idea to train everyone in the hallmarks of phishing attempts, which include:

- Trying to scare you
- Playing on your emotion
- Playing up extreme urgency

Ensure all internal processes specify that if there is ever a legitimate internal urgent email that it does not contain links and simply directs the recipient to an internal site. All internal announcements should be posted on an internal website as well.

Vulnerability Management

Siggi Bjarnason

At a super high level, the concept of vulnerability management is pretty simple. It's all about managing your vulnerabilities. When you dive deeper, then questions start to surface. Questions such as:

- What exactly is a vulnerability?
- How do I know know what my vulnerabilities are?
- Can I manage something I don't know about?

Some think that vulnerability management is all about having vulnerability scanners such as Tenable Nessus or Qualys and periodically running scans with them. Others believe it involves periodic penetration testing. Not only is this extremely flawed thinking, but it is also potentially dangerous and increases your exposure instead of reducing it.

The purpose of a good vulnerability management program is to reduce your exposure and make it easier for you to respond when an issue comes up. To answer the preceding questions, you can't manage something you don't know about. To define the word "vulnerability," turn to any English dictionary; it will give a good definition applicable here. The third question will require some discussion.

Since you can't manage what you don't know about, a good asset and configuration management is the foundation of a good vulnerability management program. If you can only do one thing, just get your hands around what you have. This, of course, starts with knowing what computers you have where, what IP addresses they have, and who is responsible for them. Know how big the hard drives are, how much memory the computers have, and what sort of NICs they have isn't critical to vulnerability management, but it is useful information to have for other programs. Knowing the media access control (MAC) addresses could come in handy though, for this discussion. Once you have the basics covered, it is time to dive deeper; this is often called configuration management, but it is just an extension of asset management. In this stage, you collect details about what is installed on each computer. Here you capture things like:

- What operating system is installed, what version, and when was it last patched?
- What applications are installed, what versions, and when were they last patched?
- What frameworks are used by what applications?
- Do any of the frameworks or applications rely on external components or modules?
- Is any of this managed by someone other than the system owner?

Notice a trend there? For good asset and configuration management, all this and more should be documented in excruciating detail.

Once you have all of this documented, it is time to turn to the process side:

- How will you stay informed with issues that come up in the industry?
- Who is going to watch announcements from US-CERT, NIST, NVD, etc.?
- How will you go about remediating issues as they are discovered? Who will have what role? How will information flow?
- Publish a statement on your website on how a security researcher can notify you of an issue they notice externally. Then have an internal process for how you handle these notices. This is called the responsible disclosure process.

Now you can say you have a vulnerability management program. Notice how there is no tool involved so far. The only tool you might think about so far is a configuration management database (CMDB). If you are a small enough org, you can do all of this with nothing more than Microsoft Office, Open Office, or Google Docs/Sheets.

Only after you've got both solid configuration management and strong policy and procedure should you even think about bringing in a vulnerability scanner.

Reduce Insider Risk Through Employee Empowerment

Stacey Champagne

According to a 2018 Ponemon Institute report, two out of three insider threat incidents were found to be due to employee or contractor negligence. The annualized cost? $3.81 million.[1]

When we dig into these cases, the "inadvertent," "accidental," or "negligent" insider typically has one of these three main excuses:

I didn't know:

- We're not supposed to use removable media devices.
- I shouldn't send business documents to my personal email.
- The CEO wouldn't ask me to purchase gift cards and respond with the barcodes.
- Who I should check with to make sure this email is legitimate.

I didn't have:

- My work laptop because I left it at my house, car, at the airport, etc.
- The application I needed on my computer to open the file.
- The time to make sure that I was doing things securely. I just needed to get this project out the door.

---

1 "2018 Cost of Insider Threats: Global Organizations." The Ponemon Institute, LLC. April 2018 (*https://oreil.ly/VpCit*).

There wasn't a way:

- To securely move my personal photos off my computer.
- To work on this document on my iPad, or easily collaborate with a colleague.
- For me to report the fact that I just saw someone not acting like themselves, exiting with a large stack of printouts under their arm.

The good news is that these excuses are addressable AND they don't necessarily require a sophisticated user behavior analytics (UBA) or data loss prevention (DLP) solution to have impact. While these technologies have a time and place within insider risk programs, and when they work they can be very helpful and effective, there are *so* many opportunities to proactively influence and set employees up to do the right thing:

I didn't know:

- *Host a webinar.* Even if nobody tunes in, record it to be available 24/7. Walk through processes like installing and registering a multifactor authentication app. Talk through properly configuring the permissions on a document intended to be shared from a cloud storage location. Employees can ask questions of you, which gives you feedback on opportunities for additional training and process improvements.
- *Set up automated travel security reminders* when employees book trips.
- *Leverage "theme months."* October is National Cybersecurity Awareness Month. There are tons of materials, talks, and events happening that you can share with your workforce without having to create content yourself.

I didn't have:

- *Make sure everyone has the help desk phone number and email* memorized, saved in their phones, or stuck somewhere on their laptop or desk.
- *Enable hotspot capabilities on employer-provided mobile phones,* so that your employees can use it when they're at hotels, airports, or other public places where the security of the networks are questionable.

There wasn't a way:

- Make sure they have a secure *way to connect to the network, print, and transfer files when working outside of the office.*

- Expect that employees are going to intermingle some personal artifacts on your devices. Give them a way *to properly ask and export that data if they need to* so that they don't use alternative methods that raise flags and create noise.

- There may be a time when an employee can't log in, and work has to get done. If employees are provided and trained *to use cloud storage and sharing platforms,* you can at least introduce a few additional mitigating controls instead of having a document sitting in someone's personal email account.

- What's the way *to report phishing emails*? What's the *way to report suspicious behaviors* that are witnessed of colleagues? How about *reporting accidental data security events,* like sending a document to the wrong recipient, or a lost device. Is it crystal clear what to report, when to report, and where to report?

Fitting Certifications into Your Career Path

Steven Becker

Obtaining a certification is simply a validation of what you know in a specific knowledge domain. While certification objectives vary, they usually include a minimum requirement of passing a multiple-choice exam, and occasionally a simulation. Some may require work experience in the subject area or require specific training courses. More advanced requirements are indicative of the certification being intended for a more advanced candidate.

Regardless of where you are in your career path, certifications play a role in proving your ability to current and potential employers and peers. Training or studying for certifications also helps level the playing field by providing a shared framework and language. Deciding on what certifications to pursue, and when, is something that will provide immense benefit. I like the three-legged stool as a way to look at your overall career growth. The three stool legs consist of formal education, certifications, and experience. If they don't work together properly, the stool wobbles or even tips over, so you have to grow each leg together to stay balanced.

Formal education can include higher education coursework, but also training that focuses on the concepts that are tested by certification exams. Experience can be trickier, because you often need the other two legs first, but training courses and home labs are certainly a part of experience. Again, keep in mind some certification requirements include experience. So how do the certifications themselves fit into your career growth? They must be relevant to what you want to achieve, but also relevant to what you already know and have done. Let's dive in more and look at what that means.

CompTIA is among the foundational certification bodies in many facets of IT for people starting their careers. The only requirement to obtain a certification is a passing exam score. While the exam objectives list experience suggestions that increase your likelihood of passing, they are not requirements.

These levels of exams, especially Security+, can be a door opener for those looking to join the information security field.

There are also more technical- and vendor- focused certifications. Cisco offers commonly sought networking certifications, but other vendors offer their own as well. Most vendor certifications are similar to CompTIA in that they normally only require passing a multiple-choice exam. eLearnSecurity provides increasingly popular practical penetration testing training and exam-based certifications for many skill levels. OSCP, from Offensive Security, is a very intensive certification that requires a 24-hour practical exam, but is respected for many technical security roles. Keep in mind it is an entry-level penetration testing certification, but pen testing is not an entry-level job!

As for management and governance, risk, and compliance (GRC) focused career paths, two common certification bodies are (ISC)^2 and ISACA. The most common certification from (ISC)^2 is CISSP, while ISACA is known for CISA, CISM, and CRISC. Both organizations offer others that are generally less technical in nature, but contain a very wide breadth of content. Work experience in the area that the exam covers is required, which makes it clear these are not designed for someone looking to break into a security career. Although it is not specifically a security certification, the Project Management Institute offers the PMP certification, which can be very beneficial for some security programs and IT cultures.

Overall, the goal of any certification is to validate your knowledge in the area you are working in or desire to. Keep that in mind, along with what you know and what you want to know, when looking for your next certification. If you do, you'll set yourself up for a rewarding, lasting career.

Phishing Reporting Is the Best Detection

Steven Becker

Phishing and email social engineering threats rank among the top attacks faced by organizations of all types. Credentials being leaked to attackers of all kinds are leveraged into business email compromise, fraudulent transactions, espionage, ransomware, and other scenarios. There are a number of security controls and products that block most spam and phishing, but getting your colleagues to report suspicious emails is critical to finding and remediating issues from the messages that still get through.

Many email-based social engineering attacks will not target a single address. If as few as 10 email addresses are targeted to an organization with a reporting rate of 10%, that means that 1 person reporting the message can help the security team locate 9 other targets, often *before* an incident occurs. Having the security team build a culture that encourages reporting suspicious messages will add to the success of an incident response team, and this scales to organizations of every size.

Building this security culture means that every suspicious message that is reported must be received willingly, and without any negative judgment. IT and security teams often have a stereotype of a gruff personality, and this must be broken by showing empathy and care to every reported message, especially when an attack may have been successful. Remember that the reporter is your colleague or customer, or maybe a friend or closer, and also a human being.

For preparation, security awareness training is critical, with an emphasis on reporting anything suspicious. Simulated phishing attacks can also provide metrics about reporting rates, but these simulations cannot lead to punitive damage for those who fall for the fake messages. Instead, consider rewarding those who report these messages through something like a random drawing for something as simple as a $5 coffee gift card. An ounce of prevention is better than a pound of cure!

After preparation, we move to detection. In addition to antispam tools, regular log reviews and threat hunting techniques are useful, but encouraging mass scale reporting is key. Each report can lead to more previously undetected messages. Every single report reviewer must use a similar, empathy-based approach, so buy your support and support staff lunch and get everyone on the same page! They are often the first humans to receive a suspicious report from someone at the organization, which moves us into recovery.

Keep in mind that intelligence isn't a factor: just a moment of distraction causes a social engineering attack to work. The person reporting an incident is a human being who fell for an increasingly sophisticated, targeted, and researched attack. Placing blame on them during incident response can lead to the reporter not providing crucial information that will help remediate the issue, such as what actually happened, what was clicked on, or what information may have been given away. Encourage ownership of a security incident to be shared by working with the victim to help identify what occurred. This will lead to more information being available to security teams to find other targets and remediate issues quickly, or even before those targets become victims.

After recovering from a potential or confirmed incident, remember it will happen again. Use these real-world examples in redacted training, and highlight positive reactions and outcomes from across the organization. Including some attacks that were thwarted due to reporting will help encourage even more reporting, and so the cycle can continue. While you may find a lot of false positives reported, that is always better than having a real incident to handle.

Know Your Data

Steve Taylor

> *There are known knowns, things we know that we know; and there are known unknowns, things that we know we don't know. But there are also unknown unknowns, things we do not know we don't know.*
> — Donald Rumsfeld

While sounding deeply philosophical and being fun to say out loud, the former Secretary's quote is quite true when it comes to information security. Whether it is logs, alerts, vulnerability scans, threat intelligence, or asset inventory, data is the life blood of a security professional. To be good at information security, you need to understand your data—both what it tells you and what it does not tell you.

Known Knowns

On the surface, your security data is usually straightforward:

- The firewall logs can tell you what source tried to connect to what destination on what port, and if a rule allowed or denied the connection.
- Reports from your vulnerability assessment tool can tell you which endpoints are missing what patches.
- Windows security log events can tell you which account logged on to a machine and the logon type used.

Fully understanding the details of what each data source can provide is key to seeing where your data overlaps. Knowing this, you can pivot across your entire data estate to make interesting deductions. Consider the case of a lateral movement risk:

- An inventory of local groups can tell you that Alice is an administrator on Workstation1 and Bob is an administrator on Server1.
- The event logs can tell you that Bob logs in to Workstation1.

- Combining those data points, we can deduce that Alice's account poses a risk to `Server1`, despite her not having direct access to it.

While that is a simple example, think about how many of your data sources contain usernames, machine names, IP addresses, etc., and the various ways you can chain those sources together to create new data points. Without a full understanding of what data each source provides, it is extremely difficult to come to those interesting conclusions.

Known Unknowns

It is also essential to know what your data does not tell you:

- Active Directory replication metadata can tell you where and when a user's `displayName` was changed.
- Event ID 4738 on the domain controller can tell you who made the change and sometimes what the new value of that attribute is.
- Combining those two data sources gives you a good idea of what happened, but neither of those sources will tell you what the old value of `displayName` was.

Fret not! Determining what your current data does not tell you is not a dead end. Knowing your data's current limitations can lead to making your data collection more robust. Can you deduce the details you are missing by parsing or correlating data you already have? Is there another data source you need to collect? Is this just a blind spot you need to document? Knowing what you don't have is a great way to determine what you need to learn next.

Unknown Unknowns

Unfortunately, I do not know what you don't know. To overcome this, all I can do is implore you to be a constant learner. The ability to learn new things may be the single most important trait for an InfoSec practitioner to have. The things you already know about protecting your infrastructure will probably still be useful in the future, but I can guarantee that you will need to learn something new—especially the limits of your new data.

Don't Let the Cybersecurity Talent Shortage Leave Your Firm Vulnerable

Tim Maliyil

According to Gartner, there were over 3.5 million open and unfilled cybersecurity positions at the end of 2020. That means that several firms worldwide feel vulnerable to a cyberattack, and they need knowledgeable team members to protect them. The reality is that these positions will never be filled. The skills gap will not be resolved by recruiting new talent. Yes, all types of schools and programs prepare people for cybersecurity careers, but there is a big gap that even the most reputable educational institutions don't fill.

It's experience.

How do I get experience if nobody will hire me without experience? I am not referring to cybersecurity-related experience. I am referring to broad technology experience. Before becoming a cybersecurity professional, you need to have a background in creating software or being a network infrastructure manager. Someone going through cybersecurity training needs to find immediate relatability to the security principles presented. Otherwise, these professionals will only be able to regurgitate techniques and policies at best.

Here are some tips for filling your firm's cybersecurity needs with your existing team:

Train your software engineers.
> Software engineers create software to solve problems. That software eventually becomes a critical part of business operations; thus, security issues can be catastrophic for continued business operations. You'd be surprised how many software engineers don't know about simple threats such as SQL injection. I was shocked that my classmates in various

security training programs did not understand the ramifications of something like SQL injection. Why? My classmates never built software, nor have they even run a SQL query.

Train your network engineers.

There is often a tendency to make network security policies lax for software processes to work. Everything is great until there is a breach. Network engineers work under stressful conditions, and that stress is relieved once the network gets out of the way of business applications. This can often lead to embarrassing security failures. Network engineers need to understand applications, and they need to work closely with application engineers to make sure the most restrictive network policies are applied.

CIOs and CTOs need to know it all.

Sorry. If you want to be at the top, you need to understand both networks and application development. Why? It will make you a more effective and respected manager, and if something terrible does happen, it will be your head on the chopping block anyway.

The one lesson I want you to gain from this article is that there is no such thing as someone who is just a cybersecurity engineer. An effective cybersecurity engineer has software development or network engineering experience and knows and understands cybersecurity principles. There is great value in being a generalist for career advancement, which is undoubtedly true in the information security space.

An organization will be most secure if everyone has cybersecurity on their mind. I recently had the privilege of teaching approximately 200 high school students basic programming, database management, and cloud infrastructure technology at Bronx Science (*https://bxscience.edu*). I made a point to bring up acceptable cybersecurity practices whenever applicable. I wanted these students to be thinking about security from the very beginning. Judging from the class participation around those topics, the security tips were often met with great interest from the students.

Having such training will make your organization a desirable destination for talented engineers, and your existing staff can leverage their institutional knowledge of your organization's infrastructure to apply changes to your security landscape quickly. Properly educating people based on their respective work experiences is the easiest way to achieve operational IT excellence with cybersecurity readiness.

Comfortable Versus Confident

Tkay Rice

In the tech industry, a common phrase you may hear often is "Fake it until you make it." This phrase has always brought a questionable expression on my face with thoughts of laziness. I would sometimes ask myself, Why spend so much time faking "it" when you can spend time actually learning "it"? Then suddenly it dawned on me: people would rather appear confident than comfortable.

The idea of being confident is to be self-assured by feeling or displaying confidence. But what does this really mean? Is it not OK to worry about a speaking engagement or to question if something you said was right? Many times, people associate not having confidence as a sign of weakness, but instead it is a sign of lack of comfortability. If you think about it, confidence and comfortability go hand in hand. Some cannot portray confidence until they are comfortable.

Is Lack of Confidence the New Imposter Syndrome?

Be aware that people may make you feel like you have imposter syndrome just because you have not displayed a level of confidence to their satisfaction. Disregard the unsolicited advice and work on how you can build your confidence through comfortability. It is better to focus on being knowledgeable in a subject because as you become more knowledgeable you will get comfortable, and that will turn into confidence. For IT (information technology) professionals, we are at the center of constantly changing or new products surfacing. If you were asked to speak on something you have not read up on, of course your confidence level would be low because you have not reached a level of comfort yet. It is important to understand that confidence is not a sign of not being sure of oneself or the fear of speaking publicly. Let us take the emotion out of the word "confidence" and address it as someone who is clearly not comfortable yet with the material.

Using Offensive/Sensitive Terms

Telling someone they are not confident enough can be a sensitive conversation to have; it is like telling someone they are not good enough to work here. Be mindful of the words you use and how they are used. Rather than using the term "confident" or confidence," say something like, "Mark, you displayed a lack of comfortability in that presentation." This would provide the speaker with information that they need to work on their comfort level by gaining more knowledge or learning ways to present effectively.

Top Three Strategies for Displaying Confidence

Great posture
    Stand up straight and relax.

Tone and delivery
    Project your voice while keeping a steady pace and pause for a few seconds to emphasize key points. Use hand gestures and show excitement with a smile.

Eye contact
    Maintain eye contact with your audience while speaking.

Keep in mind that having these strategies down pat and appearing to someone that you are confident is just part of the "fake it until you make it" persona. This persona will only get you so far and eventually lead to your downfall. If you want to be a successful IT professional, then you will need to put in the work; there are no shortcuts in life. So, the next time someone tells you or you think about telling someone to be more confident, just think about how you or they can achieve comfortability.

Some Thoughts on PKI

Tarah Wheeler

PKI or public key infrastructure is about how two entities learn to trust each other in order to exchange messages securely. You may already know that Kerberos and the KDC (Key Distribution Center) work on a shared-secrets principle, where users can go to a central authority and get authorization to communicate and act in a given network. PKI is a more complex system that understands lots of different networks in which some keys you already trust can delegate their trust (and hence yours) to other keys you don't yet know.

There are five parts of certificate or web PKI:

Certificate authorities (CAs)
> The granting bodies for public/private keys are in practice a form of verification to grease organizational wheels when there's no other method of demonstrating that you are who you say you are...a function of identity.

Registration authorities (RAs)
> These have what is essentially a license to issue certificates based on being trusted by the CA, and dependent upon their ability (which is sometimes outsourced) to validate organizational identity in a trustworthy way. CAs issue certificates, and RAs verify the information provided in those certificates.

Certificate databases
> These databases store requests for certificates as opposed to the certificates themselves.

Certificate stores
> Stores hold the actual certificates. I wasn't in charge of naming these bloody things or I'd have switched this one with certificate databases because it's not intuitive.

Key archival servers

These servers are a possible backup to the certificate database in case of some kind of disaster. This is optional and not used by all CAs.

Keys work like this: a pair of keys is generated from some kind of cryptographic algorithm, perhaps RSA (Rivest–Shamir–Adleman) or ECDSA (Elliptic Curve Digital Signature Algorithm). Think of those as wildly complicated algebraic equations that spit out an interrelated "x" string and a "y" string. You can give the "x" to anyone anywhere, and they can encrypt any message "m" with that "x." Now, while they know the original message, *only you can unencrypt the message* using your "y" key. That's why you can send the "x" key to anyone who wants to talk to you, but you should protect the secrecy of your "y" key with your teeth and nails.

The two major uses for PKI are for email and web traffic. Traffic over the internet is just a series of packets—little chunks of bits and bytes. While we think of email messages and web requests as philosophically distinct, they're basically just packets with different port addresses.

If you want to secure email back and forth between two people, the two most common forms of PKI are PGP (Pretty Good Privacy) and S/MIME (Secure/ Multipurpose Internet Mail Extensions). PGP is the first commonly used form of email encryption. Created by Phil Zimmermann and Jon Callas in the early 1990s, PGP is notoriously both secure and difficult to configure for actual human usage, but remains the standard for hypersecure communication such as with journalists or in government usage. S/MIME is the outsourced version of PKI that your email provider almost certainly uses.

The other major use for PKI is a web server authenticating and encrypting communications back and forth between a client—an SSL/TLS certificate that's installed and working when you see "https" instead of "http" at the beginning of a URL. Certificate authorities create those paired keys for websites to use to both verify that they are who they say they are, and to encrypt traffic between a client who's then been assured that they're talking to the correct web server and not a visually similar fake site created by an attacker.

Don't leave a+rwx perms on the directory with your private keys. If your web security is compromised, it's probably a sysadmin issue, not a PKI encryption issue. A new 384-bit ECDSA key isn't going to be cracked by the NSA brute-forcing it. It'll be stolen from a thumb drive at a coffee shop.

PKI has become an appliance with service providers and a functional oligopoly of certificate authorities that play well with the major browsers, which is how this technology evolved into its current form of staid usefulness.

What Is a Security Champion?

Travis F. Felder

In today's world of emerging technology, the challenge of delivering secure applications in Agile development environments is already a tall order for most enterprises. Just to make things a little more interesting, pair that with the shortage of cybersecurity staff and lack of security awareness on development teams. It should not take long for enterprises to identify the need for Security Champions to help close the gaps in their application security programs.

Not only are Security Champions best equipped to handle these challenges because of the knowledge and existing foundation of trust built from working within the development team, but these volunteers are also budget-friendly.

What Is a Security Champion?

Security Champions are volunteers that typically work within development teams as software engineers, software architects, QA engineers, or DevOps engineers. It is important for the Security Champion to sit within the development team because it allows them to easily liaison between development and security and be the voice of security.

Although the Security Champions are not expected to be subject matter experts on all things cybersecurity, they should know enough to answer basic questions and serve as a bridge between the cybersecurity and development teams.

Why Does Your Company Need Security Champions?

Security Champions are an essential part of scaling cybersecurity organization initiatives and building a strong security culture within the development teams. With a Security Champion embedded within development teams, you can ensure that systems and applications have security built in from the start as a feature of the minimal viable product. Security Champions can lead threat modeling activities, share knowledge, and help make decisions with security in mind.

What Do Security Champions Do?

Security Champions play a major role or in some cases may lead threat modeling activities with the development team. During threat modeling activities, Security Champions identify and communicate threats and security countermeasures, considering the business case and regulatory and security requirements of the application or system.

Security Champions play a vital role in improving the quality of code by ensuring static/interactive/dynamic application security testing (SAST/IAST/DAST), and open source software composition analysis activities are completed throughout the software development life cycle (SDLC). Completing code scanning activities throughout the SDLC is especially essential for Agile development teams with aggressive timelines, allowing developers to address their vulnerabilities immediately after code pushes.

Security Champions function as a conduit, enabling two-way communication between the development and cybersecurity teams. Cybersecurity knowledge shares should be regularly held to discuss new projects, the latest security vulnerabilities, and policy updates. This knowledge share is also a great forum to relay any efficiencies or gaps identified by the development teams while completing security activities through the SDLC.

How to Create a Security Champions Program?

Now that you understand the role of a Security Champion and how they improve the effectiveness of cybersecurity organizations, here is how you can create your own program:[1]

Identify the development teams
Identify development teams for each product or system within the organization.

Define responsibilities
Create clear goals for what it means to be a Security Champion.

Nominate Security Champion nominations
Work with the management of the development teams to nominate the best candidate.

Set up communication channels
Create Security Champion groups or channels on the instant messaging platforms used by your organization.

Build a knowledge base
This includes primary source of strategies, best practices, and resources related to security.

Stay engaged
Schedule workshops or lunch-and-learns to discuss security topics.

---

[1] Alexander Antukh, *Security Champions 2.0*, OWASP Bucharest AppSec 2017 (*https://oreil.ly/Woss5*).

Risk Management in Information Security

Trevor Bryant

Risk management can seem daunting and less exciting than other positions. However, it is a comprehensive program that recognizes, understands, and describes the potential risks that can impact the security and privacy of the organization's delivery of services. The program is about managing the security and privacy risks at all levels and not just the information systems. It is a complex undertaking that requires the entire organization, from leaders, planners, or managers to those developing, implementing, or analyzing. Individuals that manage risk are those that know how the business functions; the services it provides to customers, partners, and employees; how it makes money; and more. Individuals in risk management have an eagle-eye view of how the business works and comes together.

Risk management activities impact every aspect of the organization and comprise framing, assessing, responding, reducing, and monitoring. Framing risk is based on the assumptions, constraints, tolerance, properties, and trade-offs. The assumptions are how risk is assessed, responded to, and monitored. Constraints impede the ability to assess, respond, and monitor. Tolerance is the degree of uncertainty to be accepted. Examples of priorities and trade-offs are varying importance of business functions, timeframes to address risk, or trade-offs amongst different types of risks.

Assessing risk identifies weaknesses, threats, harm, vulnerabilities, or the potential thereof to determine the likelihood and impact of such risks. Responding to risk occurs after the assessment results identify a need to respond to how the risk is managed (accepted, avoided, mitigated, transferred). Reducing risks are for those risks that cannot be accepted, avoided, or transferred and are reduced by implementing the prioritization, communication, and mitigation needed to manage that risk. Monitoring risk is to verify and validate that the planned courses of action for managing those risks are in place, determining the ongoing effectiveness of response measures and other impacts to the organization by changes made.

Knowing your organization's risk management program, processes, and the types of risk they face and aim to deter can help you succeed in any role you may have by understanding how the organization functions. This information can also help with knowing where you are in the organization's processes and how your actions make an impact. The knowledge can make you a trusted and valuable member of the team and perhaps become the "go-to" person. Your role in risk management is about having the information available so that the leaders can make the best risk-informed decisions.

Risk, 2FA, MFA, It's All Just Authentication! Isn't It?

Unique Glover

I'm sure you've heard the old adage, "There's nothing new under the sun."

Technology is full of buzzwords, let's face it: "cloud," "IoT", "Agile," "holistically," "AI"—sometimes I think technology is 90% marketing and 10% practice. And, it's easy for decision makers to fall into the allure and excitement the next "it" wave promises to solve, especially when the career lifespan of CISOs average two years—that "it" starts to look very attractive to the eye.

That's when you as a practitioner earn your money. As you grow in your career and climb up that proverbial ladder, you'll invariably encounter situations where while working with decision makers, you'll be placed in a position where you'll have to discern fact from myth, and those conversations may be uncomfortable but necessary.

"Our MFA will have five pillars, we'll label it the *NextGen* MFA. Our MFA will go beyond the typical three pillars—who you are, what you have, and what you know...we'll use location and keyboard typing patterns as an authentication factor! Making it less painful for our users to access our systems" my VP spoke in a room full of his subordinates as everyone nodded their head in agreement. "Huh?" was my response. See, I knew what was being asked—achieving a security utopia of balancing sensible security with a seamless user experience, thereby creating less friction, but clearly there was confusion on the simple principles of authentication and risk profiling, and why the latter is not an authentication factor.

"That's not how it works," was my response. Immediately the room went silent and I could feel the piercing eyes like King Leonidas in the movie *300*, standing in the shadow of thousands of Persian arrows. At times like this, you can choose to remain silent, stoically nodding your head while knowing what's being said will not come into fruition, or you can speak and respond with an informed answer.

Risk profiling and user behavior analytics are indeed crucial to the authentication process, and both help to determine the appropriate assurance level for an authentication request, but are not authentication factors. Risk-based authentication, contextual authentication, or context-based authentication, as it's also referred to, uses risk signals and telemetry data collected from systems (e.g., devices, network, location) to assess the levels of risk associated with an identity, and helps determine what level of authentication is required —for example, a single factor (i.e., password) or multiple factors (i.e., biometrics, FIDO token, OTP code) to prove a digital identity.

The distinction I made in the room is that risk signals would help to determine the level of rigor required to provide an identity, but intelligence itself should not be used as a means of authentication. We wouldn't lower our defenses and give carte blanche access to resources because a keystroke pattern used during a risk assessment "looked" like a human. It's analogous to trusting a person is who they are because they selected the checkbox "I'm not a robot" without actually performing the due diligence to verify.

I wish I could say that everyone agreed and we communicated the right vision and expectations to our stakeholders. But that would not be the case, and that's OK. As a security professional, it's not about "scoring points," but about equipping decision makers with the right information to achieve a goal —information grounded by facts, not fiction, not buzzwords or fluff.

As security practitioners, I believe it is our duty to discern fact from fiction, so be informed and be empowered to inform others. Be open to learning, be confident in the knowledge you've worked tirelessly to obtain, and speak the hard truths when most are left unspoken.

Things I Wish I Knew Before Getting into Cybersecurity

Valentina Palacin

The first time I went to a security conference I felt overwhelmed. I couldn't understand a thing. One of my then coworkers told me, "Oh, don't worry, nobody does." Of course, my coworker was joking, but the joke made me feel less self-conscious about my shortcomings since a lot of attendees were in the same "learning boat" as me. With time, I also realized that at conferences, we see a lot of really cool but advanced practices that are miles away from the reality of most companies, especially on the blue-team side of security.

The problem is more acute depending on where you are in the world, but even in the US, most companies are still approaching security from a reactive perspective. The "hacker imagery" marketing for security products has been around long enough that people easily understand the benefits of buying a detection tool or carrying out black-box pen tests. However, if you start by talking about operationalizing threat intelligence, you will have a much harder time convincing management about the benefits of a more proactive, but also costly, intelligence-oriented approach.

Companies, particularly those that have enough capital, really like tools. The general belief is that for any problem there is a vendor solution that can be tried. They would rather pay for a tool that promises to fix a problem rather than implement a holistic process, built around customized open source. If a vendor says it can detect xyz, then sure it can! Let's buy it and move on to the next thing. So, if you want to take a more advanced approach, you will have to prove to them the benefits of implementing, for example, a threat hunting program to test the company's defenses. And that's the starting point only if you're lucky enough to work for a company with mature logging capabilities. You'd be surprised how many "unicorns" are out there flying completely blind. In that scenario, building visibility is going to be your square one.

Don't be discouraged by trash fires. It is really exciting to be part of an evolving security posture. Just remember that it is highly likely that you'll need to start small before getting into the most advanced and exciting practices. If you are looking to break into the industry, try to cover the basics and get familiar with the advanced practices that apply to your area of interest. Go to security conferences: you'll always find interesting content explained. Some of them even have free or paid training that you can attend. Talk to other security professionals, and learn about the problems they're facing—you might be the perfect candidate for that new opening they have. Also, engage with security communities and collaborate with open source projects. There's a lot you can learn just by collaborating with others and it will help you build your brand.

Finally, a bit of cliché but true advice: trust yourself. You can probably do whatever you set your mind to. If the task ahead of you is overwhelming you, then in all likelihood you are trying to encompass too many things at once. Divide the topic that you are trying to approach into small, consumable chunks.

Your new mantra should be the following: "Start small. Trust yourself. You can do it."

Research Is Not Just for Paper Writing

Vanessa Redman

The shy worker with glasses sits quietly in the corner, and when they feel like they have listened to enough wrong answers around the room, nonchalantly mentions what no one else has previously thought of: "The problem is with the Windows IA-32 architecture implementation; the kernel cannot reconcile what it is supposed to be accessing." Cue blank stares from the others in the room. Then the crowd cheers. The company is saved. So goes the legend of the all-knowing InfoSec professional.

For many, this perception is what keeps many from entering the industry. One might feel they are already too old because they needed to have started learning about computers when they were a child; however, there are plenty of examples of talented people who started later in life. Toni Morrison published her first book at age 40; Johnny Ramone started his band at 26. The reality is that no one is the Cyber Savior. No one knows everything there is to know about cybersecurity, and if they say they do, be wary. Information security is an incredibly large subject. So what can make you stand out among the crowd? The passion of independent research.

Most companies understand that you will not show up for an interview or your first day of work knowing all the answers. In fact, many tech companies now focus their interviews on your passions and how you will fit into the company environment, rather than your ability to create an algorithm on the fly. Often, your peers are reading about subjects in their off-time, and depending on the tempo of your org, a company might be looking for you to be doing independent research on current topics/threats. InfoSec is an incredibly dynamic industry—a heavy knowledge of the latest threats, trends, and tools is necessary to stay current. Your ability to show you are willing to keep current on the security landscape not only shows initiative but shows that the experience and skills on your resume is not your end-all be-all.

Being able to conduct research does not mean memorizing those subjects and regurgitating them at a moment's notice (though you do need to be able to speak about them, sometimes to a variety of different audiences). The key is note taking. A popular note-taking application is OneNote. It can divide subjects into notebooks, tabs, and pages. It also has a search feature, so you can have endless topics that can be referenced easily. One could create notebooks such as "Emerging Threats," "Latest Tools," or any other subject that you are interested in, or that your company is. You can easily input reference links and notes so that if someone asks you about it, you can easily bring it up, or create a briefing with it. Notes are your friend and being resourceful can make you everyone's friend. Finally, a note about social media: realize that research is not just about white papers in libraries. Social sites like Twitter and Reddit can offer great discourse on the latest attacks, hacks, and GitHub repositories from the community. If everyone is talking about it, you should probably at least be familiar with it.

InfoSec can be an intimidating industry filled with lots of technical subjects and technical experts. Being a part of the larger social community and being willing to conduct independent research can prove to everyone that you are interested in being an active member of the community. Read about the latest buzz in the community, take notes, and be welcomed!

The Security Practitioner

Wayne A. Howell Jr.

The threat landscape for security practitioners changes on a daily basis. It is critical that security professionals have an understanding of key focus areas and best practices to help organizations manage their risk. When building a new security program, practitioners should incorporate the fundamental principle of, What is the risk to the business? Every company should have a risk management plan that captures what the business should focus on, and it is our job to ensure that the business understands the risks associated with it. Risks can come from various areas such as compliance risk, business risk, open source risk, supplier risk, etc. Every business understands the cost of doing business and should have a defined place within our security program. This allows organizations to be given the guidance when needed to navigate the ever-changing security landscape.

As security practitioners, it is our duty to drive organizations to incorporate the use of security tools throughout the software development life cycle. It is critical that the risk management plan is supported by security tooling. This allows development teams to identify, classify, and remediate weaknesses found during automated analysis. Security practitioners should incorporate the use of software composition analysis (SCA), static application security testing (SAST), dynamic application security testing (DAST), and manual penetration testing (MPT) at every opportunity present to drive adoption across the enterprise. There will always be pushback when trying to adopt new security tooling, especially when impacting the Agile development process. It is imperative that we educate teams that the benefit of using these tools is in the analysis coming from the tool and not the automation that runs the analysis. Integrating security within the CI/CD pipeline helps streamline your DevSecOps tool chain.

With the explosion of social media, reputation risk is exponentially impacted. Known vulnerabilities in products spread faster than the traditional news cycle in this new digital age. Some even have an instant financial impact on businesses. We must continue to educate stakeholders on the importance of being proactive instead of reactive when dealing with security issues. A reactive organization is responding to ongoing issues as they come, whereas a proactive organization is taking necessary steps incorporating security tools to reduce weaknesses before they are live in production. A common mistake that organizations make is failing to educate the enterprise about the differences between addressing Common Vulnerabilities and Exposures (CVEs) and addressing Common Weakness Enumeration (CWE). Organizations focusing solely on addressing CVEs will always be in a reactive state as opposed to focusing on reducing weaknesses identified in software, firmware, or hardware as teams are building their applications.

As we take the oath of protecting company assets, we should remember to strategically focus on identifying cybersecurity business risk. We must push stakeholders to invest in building strong automated inspection capabilities from when the first line of code is written. We must drive enterprise adoption of reducing weaknesses in software and firmware. To implement these, we need to invest in great security professionals, whether externally sourced or by building the desired competencies with strategic internal development plans. Security should never be an afterthought at any organization.

Threat Intelligence in Two Steps

Xena Olsen

Simply put, threat intelligence involves understanding threats and helping leadership make informed security decisions. Threat intelligence isn't just about novel threats or state-nexus threat actors. It is also about understanding simple attacks specific to your organization's infrastructure, controls, and detection and getting good at defending against those.

Threat intelligence doesn't have to be hard. Many organizations set unrealistic expectations for their threat intelligence teams, and I am here to tell you one thing: keep it simple. Step one: understand the people, process, and technology of your threat intelligence role. Step two: solve other people's problems. Champion a project that can build political capital and address the pain points of the security department.

Threat intelligence isn't just for large enterprise companies. Threat intelligence is for small businesses, solopreneurs, medium-sized businesses, and individuals too. All that is necessary is to broaden your perspective of what threat intelligence means to you. In a small business and solopreneur context, it can mean understanding your business's threat landscape so you can make informed decisions on how to run your business.

Step One: Understand Your Role

The people

Threat intelligence is about people. When you strip away the expensive security tools and security team, threat intelligence becomes about building relationships with intel analysts and security professionals at other companies. In small business, threat intelligence involves building relationships with other small business owners and sharing attacker tactics.

The process

Threat intelligence can help an organization prioritize threats and attacker techniques specific to its threat landscape. Purple teams rely on threat intelligence to help them prioritize threats with the intent, capability, and opportunity to attack an organization, ranging from ransomware and eCrime to state-nexus actors.

The technology

Threat intelligence isn't just about publicly available threat actor reports. An organization can draw from a combination of internal attack data, industry vertical attack data, sharing group data, publicly available threat actor reports, open source intelligence, and more. A great resource to start with understanding organization-specific attacks is to look at your email attack data, the blocked and delivered campaigns. We could get into a debate on whether or not blocked attack data is valuable, but for simplicity's sake, let's just say that we are on the same page that you can get value from blocked attacks. See how your organization holds up against the common attacks because many attackers will attempt to take the easy path.

Step Two: Solve Someone Else's Problem

The Stakeholders

Threat intelligence isn't just about MITRE ATT&CK. Not all threat intelligence reporting requires in-depth technical analysis. Instead, I recommend focusing on stakeholder intelligence requirements and serving your customers' needs. Your job is to provide value to the organization and your stakeholders. If you can't do that, your intelligence program will not last long.

The Problems

Most importantly, your job as a threat intelligence professional is to have a healthy respect for your enemies' capabilities and operations while also focusing on prevention and detection. It takes consistent creative out-of-the-box thinking along with the ability to see from the attacker's perspective to succeed in cybersecurity as a threat intelligence professional.

Threat intelligence is one of the most exciting jobs on the planet. If you pursue a career in threat intelligence, I highly recommend being comfortable with psychology and technology as threat intelligence blends both.

Maintaining Compliance and Information Security with Blue Team Assistance

Yasmin Schlegel

The terms "information security" and "compliance" go hand in hand when it comes to safeguarding information systems and protecting information. One of the first things that a person in information security and/or cybersecurity should be aware of is the importance of compliance and information security policies on information security and security posture in an organization.

The definition of information security is the process or practices that are created and implemented to protect all information systems platforms, no matter the form or classification level, from unauthorized access, disruption, modification, disclosure, deletion, or destruction. One area of compliance can be establishing a compliance program that institutes risk-based controls that protect the CIA (confidentiality, integrity, and availability) of all data stored, processed, and transferred. Information security policies in an organization are the high-level policies established for protecting people and company assets.

Part of defending against attacks on company assets, systems, and people comes with testing the environment. The blue team functions as an internal security team in an organization that protects against both red team offensive activities and real outside cyberattackers. Blue team's primary goal is to stay vigilant against potential threats and attacks that could impact the organization's systems or networks. Blue team members must have the mindset of a defender and deep-thinking skills with attack experience to simulate potential enemy attacks. Blue team members with this combination of skills can assist an organization in having a robust security posture.

Blue team exercises and activities can help an organization select the best security controls and construct a robust risk management and audit program. Blue team exercises that deal with perimeter security method configuration, security software configuration, network segmentation, least-privilege access implementation, network logging, and DNS research are all pertinent areas to ramping up an organization's security posture. Blue team activities can bring awareness of potential vulnerabilities and threats in compliance and applicability of security controls in the following National Institute of Standards and Technology (NIST) 800.171 Control Families: Access Management, Configuration Management, Identification & Authentication, Audit & Accountability, Systems & Communications Protection, and System & Information Integrity.

Governance, risk, and compliance (GRC) professionals can take security assessments completed by blue team members and apply the lessons learned to their current policies, procedures, security controls, risk management, and audit programs to address security gaps. Blue team members are technical professionals responsible for preventing, detecting, and remediating security risks to an organization. Their activities and exercises are essential to address security concerns within an organization while maintaining a vigilant security posture.

As a security professional, it is critical to understand the relationship an organization has with blue team members. They are part of the internal defense and are vital in preparing an organization for an external audit or security assessment. The overall organizational relationship with the blue team is crucial to safeguard and protect company systems and assets. Without the collaboration of the blue team and GRC professionals, an organization will stay behind on mediating security risks.

Contributors

Alyssa Columbus

Alyssa Columbus is a member of the Spring 2018 Class of NASA Datanauts, and her technical guides, tutorials, and articles have been featured by leading organizations, including *Forbes*, Microsoft, and the Association for Computing Machinery (ACM). Previously, Columbus has worked as an information security analyst, data scientist, and machine learning researcher, and she is a former contributor to open source software with over 45 million downloads. Columbus is the founder of R-Ladies Irvine and holds a degree in Mathematics from the University of California, Irvine.

Continuously Learn to Protect Tomorrow's Technology, page 1

Andrew Harris

Andrew Harris is CrowdStrike's Sr. Director for Public Sector Technology Strategy. He is responsible for driving innovation and ensuring technical alignment for the Public Sector and for emerging technologies. Prior to joining CrowdStrike, Andrew worked at Microsoft as a Principal Program Manager, where he focused on engineering solutions across 50+ engineering teams for $1B major government contracts. He served as the CTO for the Customer Experience Engineering (CxE) team for Microsoft Azure's security products and services, helping to drive strategy on those products and deliver deep customer enablement. Andrew led the Recovery team at Microsoft for Incident Response and helped NIST write the playbook on SP 800-184, "Guide for Cybersecurity Event Recovery." In addition, Andrew served as a Special Advisor to the White House, US House of Representatives, multiple Services within the Department of Defense, Pentagon, and various Fortune 100 companies. Prior to Microsoft, Andrew was a DoD civilian and was the Chief of Strategic Programs at the Defense Information Systems Agency (DISA), pioneering many programs, most of which are fully deployed and remain top priorities for the Pentagon.

Fight in Cyber like the Military Fights in the Physical, page 3

Ann Johnson

Ann Johnson is Corporate Vice President of SCI Business Development at Microsoft (*https://oreil.ly/pxrAp*). She oversees the investment and strategic partner strategy for security, compliance, and identity for one of the largest tech companies on our planet to help organizations become operationally resilient on their digital transformation journey and unlock capabilities of Microsoft's intelligent cloud and next-generation AI. She is an active member of numerous cybersecurity board of directors, and also serves as a board advisor on cybersecurity. For more about Microsoft's Cybersecurity Solutions, visit the Microsoft Security Site (*https://oreil.ly/pv6md*), or follow Microsoft Security on Twitter at Msft Security Twitter (*https://oreil.ly/YBADk*) or Msft WDSecurity Twitter (*https://oreil.ly/0cvN0*). You can also hear her talk with some of the biggest influencers in cybersecurity each week on Afternoon Cyber Tea with Ann Johnson (*https://oreil.ly/TQ1le*).

InfoSec Professionals Need to Know Operational Resilience, page 9

Antoine Middleton

Antoine Middleton is a cybersecurity practitioner and all-around tech guy. He is experienced in cloud security for public and government cloud platforms, risk assessments, Python scripting, vulnerability management, and identity and access management. Antoine holds a master's degree in Cyber and Information Security and has been in information technology for over 15 years and counting. Outside of work, he can be found helping others grow in their careers in cybersecurity and challenging his own growth by playing various instruments.

Taking Control of Your Own Journey, page 11

Ben Brook

Ben Brook is the CEO and CoFounder of Transcend, an engineering company that powers better data privacy for companies like Robinhood, Patreon, and Indiegogo. Transcend is backed by Accel and Index Ventures. *ben@transcend.io*

Security, Privacy, and Messy Data Webs: Taking Back Control in Third-Party Environments, page 13

Ben Smith

Ben Smith (@Ben_Smith) is an information security and risk management professional. His career stops include RSA Security, UUNET, and the US government, along with several technology startups. He is an acknowledged contributor to NIST SP 1800-1, -3, and -7; he holds industry certifications in information security (CCISO, CISSP), risk management (CRISC), and privacy (CIPT); and he is an appointed member of the Cybersecurity Canon Committee. Smith has presented internationally at cybersecurity events sponsored by Gartner, FS-ISAC, SANS, IANS, CERT/SEI, RSAC, ISSA, (ISC)², ISACA, Infosecurity, BSides, ASIS, InfraGard, HTCIA, SecureWorld, ISMG, SC Media, SIRA, RMA, IIA, MWCA, ICI, and other organizations.

Every Information Security Problem Boils Down to One Thing, page 15
And in This Corner, It's Security Versus the Business!, page 17
Don't Overlook Prior Art from Other Industries, page 19
Powerful Metrics Always Lose to Poor Communication, page 21

Brian Gibbs

For over 20 years, Brian Gibbs has been a noteworthy leader in the information technology and cybersecurity space. He is active on social media, video blogging, and sharing his experiences with organizations. As a vCISO, he consults with organizations to understand their critical data and develop strategies to protect it. He holds an MBA from Indiana Wesleyan University and is pursuing his Master's in Cybersecurity at Georgia Institute of Technology, where he also is a teaching assistant.

He has obtained his CISSP from (ISC)^2 and Security+ from CompTIA in addition to other certifications from Microsoft and VMware.

"No" May Not Be a Strategic Word, page 23

Camille Stewart

Camille Stewart is an industry-recognized cybersecurity authority with experience building programs and solutions to address complex technology, cyber and national security, and foreign policy challenges across the public and private sectors. Named the Head of Security and Privacy Policy for Google Play and Android, Camille leads security, privacy, election integrity, and dis/misinformation efforts for Google's mobile business. Prior to Google, Camille managed cybersecurity, election security, tech innovation, and risk issues at Deloitte. Camille was appointed by President Barack Obama to be the Senior Policy Advisor for Cyber Infrastructure and Resilience Policy at the Department of Homeland Security. Her professional achievements have earned her recognition from a multitude of entities throughout her career, including being selected as 2020 Cyber Fellow at the Harvard Kennedy School Belfer Center for Science and International Affairs and the 2019 Cyber Security Women of the Year in the "Barrier Breaker" category. You can find out more about Camille and her current projects at *www.camilleste-wart.com* and follow her on Twitter @CamilleEsq.

Keep People at the Center of Your Work, page 25

Catherine J. Ullman

Dr. Catherine J. Ullman is a security researcher, speaker, and Senior Information Security Forensic Analyst at University at Buffalo with over 20 years of highly technical experience. In her current role, Cathy is a digital forensics and incident response (DFIR) specialist, performing incident management, intrusion detection, investigative services, and personnel case resolution in a dynamic academic environment. She additionally builds security awareness among faculty and staff via a department-wide program that educates and informs users about how to prevent and detect social engineering threats, and how to compute and digitally communicate safely. Cathy has presented at numerous information security conferences, including DEF CON and Hacker Halted. In her (minimal) spare time, she enjoys visiting her adopted two-toed sloth Flash at the Buffalo Zoo, researching death and the dead, and learning more about hacking things to make the world a more secure place.

Take a Beat: Thinking Like a Firefighter for Better Incident Response, page 27
A Diverse Path to Better Security Professionals, page 29

Chase Pettet

 Chase Pettet is an information technology architecture and security professional with experience managing and mentoring teams. An emphasis on risk-informed decision making, tactical optimism, perseverance, and fostering healthy cultures of collaboration has enabled his success. He has worked for companies behind globally ranked top 10 and 150 websites for a decade in these capacities, as well as enterprises in highly regulated industries. He is a lifelong builder and continuous learner who can often be found in the workshop. He lives in the midwestern portion of the US with his wife and two daughters.

It's Not About the Tools, page 31

Chloé Messdaghi

 Chloé Messdaghi is an award-winning changemaker who is innovating tech and information security sectors to meet today's and future demands by accelerating startups and providing solutions that empower organizations and people to stand out from the crowd. She is an international keynote speaker at major information security and tech conferences and events, and serves as a trusted source to reporters and editors, such as *Forbes* and *Business Insider*. Additionally, she is one of *Business Insider*'s 50 Power Players. Outside of her work, she is the cofounder of Hacking is NOT a Crime and We Open Tech, and curator for Open Tech Pledge.

- Twitter: @ChloeMessdaghi
- LinkedIn: *https://www.linkedin.com/in/chloemessdaghi*
- Website: *https://www.chloemessdaghi.com*

Four Things to Know About Cybersecurity, page 33

Christina Lang

Christina Lang has been an Identity and Access Management (IAM) specialist since 2018, after graduating from Michigan State University (MSU). She has a strong background in federated login, tokens, secure data storage, and identity. Currently, she works to integrate secure authentication and authorization processes.

Vetting Resources and Having Patience when Learning Information Security Topics, page 36

Christina Morillo (Author/Editor of This Book)

Christina Morillo is an information security, "cybersecurity," and technology leader with an extensive background in enterprise security, identity and access management, security and IT operations, and cloud. In her current role, she leads the cloud security assessment service for Microsoft Cloud Services, including Azure Active Directory and Microsoft 365. As a strategic thinker who thrives on solving complex problems, her experience has taken her to companies such as Microsoft, Morgan Stanley, and Fitch Ratings. By demystifying security and technology, she hopes to make security accessible, approachable, and digestible, with the overarching goal of keeping people and organizations safe and secure.

Focus on the What and the Why First, Not the Tool, page 38

Damian Finol

Damian Finol has worked for over 25 years on systems hardening, risk assessments, applied cryptography (PKI/HSMs), identified insider threats and vulnerabilities, deployed security orchestration, and developed security software automation for Fortune 500 companies. Damian has also managed teams of security engineers, business analysts, security software developers, site reliability engineers (SREs), and program managers to lead the successful execution of the deployment of complex security controls at massive scale (> 100,000 people and assets). Holding a BsC and Master's in Computer Science, Damian has also been an instructor for the O'Reilly "Agile for SRE"

(*https://oreil.ly/6XErR*) class, showcasing Agile improvements within the site reliability space.

Insiders Don't Care for Controls, page 40

Dane Bamburry

 Dane Bamburry is a technology leader with over 20 years of experience. Dane currently serves as the Director of Solutions Architecture Identity and Access Management, and Enterprise Content Management at Cox Enterprises, Inc. Bamburry has a bachelor's degree in Management Information Systems from the University of Notre Dame and an Organizational Leadership MBA from Ashford University. Currently, he serves on the Board of Directors of ITSMF, which increases the representation of black professionals at senior levels in technology, and on the Georgia State University CIS Advisory Board.

Identity and Access Management: The Value of User Experience, page 42

Danny Moules

 Danny "Rushyo" Moules is a hacker and law student who has worked as a consultant to governments and businesses across the world, both red and blue, technical and management. They have worked on pro bono legal projects and are in the final modules of their QLD. They are currently taking an extended break from the InfoSec industry working for the British National Health Service on clinical systems.

Lessons from Cross-Training in Law, page 44

David McKenzie

 David is a cybersecurity and information technology executive with 23 years of experience, specializing in IT and cybersecurity managed services. David is Head of Managed Services at Quorum Cyber; with headquarters in Edinburgh, Quorum Cyber provides managed cyber defense services for customers across multiple industries. Previous roles and responsibilities include Principal Consultant in Managed Services, Senior Technical Consultant, and Senior Incident Responder. David notes, "I believe that security or technology failed the user, not the other way around. I believe that all companies, regardless of size, deserve to have the capabilities to keep their employees and business safe from cyberattack. I believe that we all have a responsibility to give back to our communities and help protect them. I want my customers to be able to concentrate on their business while trusting my team to man the walls. Blue team through and through. Protect the people, build the walls, man the walls, stare the bad guys in the eye, shrug and tell them—Bring it." David can be reached via Twitter @davewj.

Ransomware, page 46

Dominique West

Dominique West is currently a Technical Account Manager and creator of the Security in Color cybersecurity podcast. Achieving her CISSP, MS in Cybersecurity and currently pursuing a Doctorate in Business Administration, Dominique is deeply passionate about cloud security and cyber awareness, with nine years of experience in IT spanning risk, vulnerability, incident and response, cloud transformation, and security across commercial industries. In addition to her professional endeavors, she founded Security in Color, a digital education platform aimed at building the next generation of cybersecurity champions. She has a weekly podcast and newsletter, of the same name, that provides the top national cybersecurity news and resources in an easily digestible format. Additionally, Dominique leads and volunteers with various women in technology groups and currently serves as the Chief of Membership Engagement for the Women's Society of Cyberjutsu, a nationwide nonprofit. To connect with Dominique, you can find her via the following social media platforms or by email:

- Twitter and Instagram: @Domyboo, @securityincolor
- Website: *www.securityincolor.com*
- Linkedin: *https://www.linkedin.com/in/dominiquewest*
- Podcast: *https://anchor.fm/sic*

The Key to Success in Your Cloud Journey Begins with the Shared Responsibility Model, page 48

Fernando Ike

Fernando Ike has worked in various companies, including startups, media, telecom, banks, and IT. He has taken on different roles like CTO, IT Manager, Developer Advocate, Sysadmin, and Consultant. He was also a volunteer for open source projects like Debian and PostgreSQL, and he's co-organizer of DevOpsDays Sao Paulo.

Why InfoSec Practitioners Need to Know About Agile and DevOps, page 50

Frank McGovern

Frank McGovern is a cybersecurity aficionado in Chicago, Illinois with over a decade of experience. Frank has experience working in cybersecurity architecture, design, implementation, GRC (policy, risk management, and compliance tracking), and more. He has specialization in the Microsoft E5 product stack. Frank also cofounded Blue Team Con, a cybersecurity conference for defenders of enterprises, is involved in the automotive detailing industry, and loves to play video games.

The Business Is Always Right, page 53

Gleydson Mazioli da Silva

Gleydson Mazioli da Silva (*gleydson@guiafoca.org*) is cofounder and CIO at SpiritSec and author of Guia Foca (a free guide that has been the most used Linux and security guide in Portuguese-language countries since 1999). Gleydson is passionate for DevOps, automation, and securing things, and is a LPI 303, 304 certified professional and IOT Enthusiast.

Why Choose Linux as Your Secure Operating System?, page 55

Guillaume Blaquiere

Guillaume has been a Google Developer Expert on the Cloud Platform since 2019 and works at Sfeir as a Cloud Architect. As a Java developer for more than 15 years, and despite positions of responsibility, he has always kept his wish to create, develop, discover, and test new solutions, especially in the cloud, in machine learning, and in the Python and Go languages. Innovation addict and Google Cloud 3x certified, writer and speaker in his free time, he's fascinated by the serverless solution and all the "usual" problems that it solves. More generally, he likes helping people stuck on Google Cloud; you can find him on Stack Overflow (guillaume-blaquiere), Medium (@guillaume-blaquiere), and Twitter (@gblaquiere).

New World, New Rules, Same Principles, page 57

Guy Lépine

Guy Lépine is the Lead Developer of Security Products at Sherweb, a world-class cloud service provider. He is also deeply involved in the undergraduate specialization in security given at the computer engineering department of the University of Sherbrooke. During his 25 years in the software development industry, Guy has always had an acute interest in computer security, which led him to obtain a master's degree specialized in network protocol security, graduating while working in various software development businesses. Having been trained in the Canadian Armed Forces as a Communications Engineer, Guy has always known the value of data protection.

Data Protection: Impact on Software Development, page 59

Gwyneth Peña-Siguenza

Gwyneth Peña-Siguenza is a Cloud Advocate at Microsoft and a YouTuber. She enjoys using her experience in cloud and content creation to further develop the community knowledge base and encourage others with a nontraditional background to pursue a career in this space.

An Introduction to Security in the Cloud, page 62

Gyle dela Cruz

Gyle had an interesting path to InfoSec. She completed a degree in psychology and spent a couple of years in law school before shifting to tech. After several years of working on networks in technical support and training delivery, she moved into specializing in InfoSec. She completed her Graduate Certificate in Incident Response from The SANS Institute and a Master's in Cyber Security-Digital Forensics from UNSW Canberra, ADFA. She now works as a Cyber Threat Analyst and loves using her skills and knowledge to help protect and defend organizations and people. She also volunteers for different community-based organizations and events.

Knowing Normal, page 65

Harshvardhan Parmar

Harshvardhan Parmar is the Global Head of Data Science for Atos MDR. His work involves establishing the vision and mission of using data science to detect advanced cybersecurity threats and overseeing the creation of cutting-edge artificial intelligence (AI) models and various scoring algorithms used in AIsaac, Atos's next-gen AI platform used for delivering managed detection and response (MDR) services. Harshvardhan has been working in the information security domain for over 12 years, during which he has directly serviced large enterprises and Fortune 500 customers in the US and Europe and Asia-Pacific region. He is a Certified Information Systems Auditor, and currently holds two US patents in AI and cybersecurity.

Threat Hunting Based on Machine Learning, page 157

Ian Barwise

Ian Barwise has over 25 years of professional experience in IT system administration, information assurance, security control assessments, and network security engineering during a career in the US Marine Corps and also from time spent working in the private sector. Ian holds a BSc degree in Information System Security with a concentration in Digital Forensics and a MSc degree in Cybersecurity Studies both from the American Military University. He also holds the Certified Information System Security Professional

(CISSP), the Certified Ethical Hacker (CEH), the Certified Network Defense Architect, and the Security+ce certifications. Ian resides in Los Angeles, California with his family.

All Signs Point to a Schism in Cybersecurity, page 67

Idan Plotnik

Idan Plotnik is the cofounder and CEO of Apiiro, a serial entrepreneur, and a cybersecurity product strategist. Previously, Idan was Director of Engineering at Microsoft following the acquisition of Aorato, where he served as the founder and CEO.

DevSecOps Is Evolving to Drive a Risk-Based Digital Transformation, page 69

Jam Leomi

Jam Leomi (pronouns: they/them) has worked in the tech industry for over 15 years and is currently Lead Security Engineer at Honeycomb. With a degree in Information Assurance and Security Engineering, Jam has lent a keen eye towards security, operations, and systems engineering at companies like Google, CloudPassage, and GitHub. In their spare time they make music, delicious food, and pens!! You can find them on twitter as @jamfish728, where they usually rant about the world, and sometimes tech.

Availability Is a Security Concern Too, page 71

James Bore

James, after nearly two decades in security (and a bit of time when it was uncertain whether he was in security or IT), runs his own cybersecurity consultancy along with working as an instructor to bring more people into the fold and occasionally running virtual community events and conferences. Along with the traditional security interests of lockpicking, scripting, and cryptography he is an amateur butcher, brewer, and beekeeper (just to keep the bee theme going) and regularly speaks at events. Finally, he is always open to ask for help or approaches with interesting information.

Security Is People, page 73

Jasmine M. Jackson

Jasmine Jackson has a master's degree in Computer Science and a graduate certificate in Information Security and Privacy from the University of North Carolina. Currently, she works at AvidXChange as an Application Security Engineer II. In her spare time, she likes to spoil her fur babies, Stormy and Skylar, stay up to date on security vulnerabilities by completing capture the flags, and play video games on her RetroPie. To reach her, follow her on Twitter or Instagram at @thefluffy007.

Penetration Testing: Why Can't It Be Like the Movies?!, page 75

Jeff Luszcz

Jeff Luszcz was the Founder of Palamida, one of the first open source discovery and vulnerability management companies, a field now called Software Composition Analysis. Since 2004, he has helped hundreds of software companies understand how to best use open source while complying with their license obligations and keeping on top of security issues. He and his team have performed reviews for some of the largest mergers and acquisitions in the technology industry. He consults with companies on the topics of compliance, remediation, and security. He shares his thoughts on the industry at zebracatzebra.com and is a frequent conference speaker.

Understanding Open Source Licensing and Security, page 79

JR Aquino

JR has a rich history of building security departments and security programs for some of the largest and highly regulated cloud service providers in the industry. He is currently the Principal Product Security Program Manager working in the Azure Edge Team at Microsoft. Prior to his current role, JR led the Security Incident Response team for Microsoft's Cloud and AI Division, including Azure and Dynamics 365. At Citrix Systems he established the security program for the GoTo products (GoToMeeting,

GoToMyPC, GoToWebinar). At LCOGT, JR architected the global network of robotic telescopes controlled over the internet for astronomy research.

Planning for Incident Response Customer Notifications, page 81

Julie Agnes Sparks

Julie Agnes Sparks is a Security Engineer at Cloudflare working on the Detection and Response Team. She graduated from Rollins College in Orlando, FL with a degree in Computer Science, History, and Economics. Julie Agnes is actively involved in the Women in Cybersecurity (WiCyS) organization as a committee member, mentor, and mentee. She is interested in the interdisciplinary nature of security, especially as it relates to disinformation networks, privacy, transparency, and inclusion. In addition to her professional work, Julie Agnes focuses on learning new things, buying copious amounts of books, traveling to new places, and taking time to connect with nature.

Managing Security Alert Fatigue, page 84

Karen Scarfone

Karen Scarfone is the principal consultant for Scarfone Cybersecurity in Clifton, Virginia. She develops cybersecurity publications for government agencies, security vendors, media companies, and other organizations. Karen has worked in information technology for nearly 30 years, with over 20 years of that dedicated to security. She holds a bachelor's degree in computer science from the University of Wisconsin-Parkside, a master's degree in computer science from the University of Idaho, and a master's degree in technical writing from Utah State University.

Take Advantage of NIST's Resources, page 86

Keirsten Brager

Keirsten Brager is a Sr. Security Consultant specializing in ICS/OT. She has a master's degree in Cybersecurity and several industry certifications, including the GICSP and CISSP. Keirsten is passionate about helping women earn more money, so she published *Secure The InfoSec Bag: Six Figure*

Career Guide for Women in Security (https://oreil.ly/gYMnY). She produced this resource to help underestimated talent negotiate better total compensation packages, diversify their incomes, and close their own pay gaps.

Apply Agile SDLC Methodology to Your Career, page 88

Kelly Shortridge

Kelly Shortridge is currently VP of Product Management and Product Strategy at Capsule8. Kelly is coauthor of the *Security Chaos Engineering* report published by O'Reilly, and is a frequent speaker, advisor, and consultant on the applications of behavioral economics to information security as well as the intersection of DevOps and InfoSec. Previously, Kelly managed products at SecurityScorecard and BAE Systems Applied Intelligence after cofounding and serving as COO of IperLane, an enterprise security startup that was acquired.

Failing Spectacularly, page 90

Kim Z. Dale

Kim Z. Dale is an information security policy specialist and writer whose experience includes financial services, government, logistics, and higher ed.

The Solid Impact of Soft Skills, page 92

Lauren Zink

Lauren Zink is an industry-recognized information security professional who has developed, expanded, and maintained security awareness programs. Her recognitions include: IFSEC Global Influencer in Cybersecurity, Women in IT Awards Finalist-Young Leader of the Year, Stark County 20 Under 40, Women in IT Awards Finalist-Security Champion of the Year, Cyber Educator of the Year-Women's Society of Cyberjutsu, Influential Woman in Tech by Crain's Cleveland, and Women in IT: Honorable Mention by SC Magazine. Most recently, Lauren was a contributor to *Rise of the Cyber Women: Volume One*. Lauren is also a LinkedIn Learning author of two security courses and has been published in numerous industry magazines and websites. She is a great advocate for women in STEM, volunteering her time mentoring women as well as talking at schools, businesses, and conferences.

What Is Good Cyber Hygiene Within Information Security?, page 94
Phishing, page 96
Building a New Security Program, page 98

Lee Atchison

Lee Atchison is a recognized industry thought leader in cloud computing, and the author of the best-selling book *Architecting for Scale*, published by O'Reilly Media, currently in its second edition. Lee has 33 years of industry experience, including eight years at New Relic and seven years at Amazon.com and AWS, where he led the creation of the company's first software download store, created AWS Elastic Beanstalk, and managed the migration of Amazon's retail platform to a new service-based architecture. Lee has consulted with leading organizations on how to modernize their application architectures and transform their organizations at scale. Lee is an industry expert and is widely quoted in publications such as *InfoWorld*, *Diginomica*, *IT Brief*, *Programmable Web*, *CIO Review*, and *DZone*. He has been a featured speaker at events across the globe from London to Sydney, Tokyo to Paris, and throughout North America.

Using Isolation Zones to Increase Cloud Security, page 100

Lodrina Cherne

Lodrina Cherne is a champion for security in the digital forensics and cybersecurity industries. As Principal Security Advocate at Cybereason, she drives innovation and development of best practices related to cybersecurity standards and policy. Cherne is also a Certified Instructor at the SANS Institute where she helps information security professionals advance their foundational understanding of digital forensics. Cherne's role as a Researcher at the Technology and Social Change Project at Harvard Kennedy School's Shorenstein Center also works to frame technology in the public discourse about the reliability of information online. Cherne has earned a bachelor's degree in Computer Science from Boston University and has participated in the TELI program at Aspen Tech Policy Hub.

If It's Remembered for You, Forensics Can Uncover It, page 103

Louis Nyffenegger

Louis Nyffenegger is the founder and director of Pentester-Lab.com, an innovative penetration testing and application security training platform trusted by thousands of industry professionals. Louis has over 15 years of experience in information security, and before founding PentesterLab worked in many technical information security roles both as a consultant and on internal teams performing code review, penetration testing, and security automation. Louis is a sought-after speaker and trainer at security conferences around the world.

Certifications Considered Harmful, page 105

Mansi Thakar

Mansi Thakar (@mansimusa) is often referred to by others as the Doctor of Digital Hygiene, and considers herself to be perpetually somewhere between a n00b and a veteran. A believer of lifting while climbing, Thakar is a leader of nonprofits that amplify technical skill sets and promote diversity. She also plays a lead role in the PBS documentary *Life Hackers* and spends her summers protecting the "most hostile network on the planet" as a DEF-CON NOC Goon. When she isn't discussing InfoSec, she can be found attempting new recipes in the kitchen and new poses on the yoga mat.

Security Considerations for IoT Device Management, page 107

Maresa Vermulst

Maresa Vermulst is a security system specialist at KPN, the Netherlands. Through online webinars, courses, a great deal of curiosity, and a tendency for breaking stuff, she managed to gather experience in the field of information security and eventually find a job. She is grateful to everyone who was willing to share their knowledge and to the online communities where so many offer guidance and advice. Her goal is to give back to the community, help others on their journey, and get more people interested in the field, as sharing is the way forward.

Finding Your Voice, page 111

Mari Galloway

Mari Galloway is an award-winning CEO and a founding board member of the Women's Society of Cyberjutsu (WSC), one of the fastest-growing 501c3 nonprofit cybersecurity communities bringing more women and girls to cyber. Mari's career began with Accenture as a Network Engineer. With over 11 years of information technology and cyber experience, her career has spanned all domains of cyber in both government and commercial industries. She holds a variety of technical and management certifications as well as a bachelor's and master's degree in Computer Information Systems. She regularly contributes to security blogs and training companies across the country and is an Adjunct Professor at University of Maryland Global Campus (UMGC). Mari also enjoys arts, puzzles, and Legos! @marigalloway | *www.linkedin.com/in/themarigalloway*

Best Practices with Vulnerability Management, page 113

Marina Ciavatta

Marina graduated with a degree in journalism and turned into a Human Hacker—she is a Brazilian Social Engineer, specializing in Physical Pentest and Information Security Awareness. As an instructor, she teaches people to better protect themselves from her own Human Hacking attacks, and much more. Marina has spoken at many hacking and InfoSec events such as the 8.8 Lovelace hacking conference, Layer 8, and HushCon.

Social Engineering, page 115

Martijn Grooten

Martijn Grooten worked as an academic mathematician before finding himself with a job at a security company almost 14 years ago. He has a broad interest in security and was the editor of Virus Bulletin for almost six years. He is a regular public speaker and writer and currently works as a security consultant with a particular focus on helping vulnerable groups and people. He is a fellow of the Civilsphere Project and a special advisor to the Coalition Against Stalkerware.

Stalkerware: When Malware and Domestic Abuse Coincide, page 117

Dr. Meg Layton

Dr. Margaret Meiman (Meg) Layton is currently serving in the role of Director of Security Architecture and Engineering for Children's National Hospital in Washington, DC. It was her work as Director of IT for a telecommunications company doing business in Africa that helped her to discover her passion for security (and her passion for travel!) at the height of the dot-com era. Meg has been a regular speaker at conferences, both nationally and internationally, on technical and security-related topics, and can be heard occasionally on technical podcasts, such as a recent interview on networking fundamentals by ITSPmagazine. You can find her on Twitter @vamegabyte and on LinkedIn: *www.linkedin.com/in/meglayton*.

Understanding and Exploring Risk, page 119

Melanie Ensign

Melanie Ensign is the founder and CEO of Discernible Inc., a specialized security and privacy communications consultancy. After managing security and privacy communications for some of the world's most notable brands including Facebook, Uber, and AT&T, she now helps even more organizations adopt effective communication strategies that improve operations and help reduce risk. She counsels executives and technical teams alike on how to cut through internal politics, dysfunctional inertia, and meaningless metrics. Melanie also leads the press department for DEF CON, the world's largest hacker conference. She holds an undergraduate degree in communications from the University of Illinois-Chicago and a Master of Science in Public Relations from Boston University.

The Psychology of Incident Response, page 121

Michael Weber

Michael Weber is a computer consultant, and working professional in various technological fields. With 25 years of formal and informal study, he is always looking for greater information adventures and loves to solve problems.

Priorities and Ethics/Morality, page 123

Michelle Ribeiro

Michelle Ribeiro is the CEO at SPIRITSEC, a Brazilian cybersecurity company, and is involved in different open source communities such as the DevOpsDays and the Debian Project. She acted as a Tech Policy Advisor for governmental initiatives and has a B side, dedicated to research at the intersection of International Security and Technology, with a focus on cyber conflicts. Michelle has pursued her master's degree in International Studies and Diplomacy at SOAS, University of London, funded by the British FCO, through a Chevening Scholarship.

DevSecOps: Continuous Security Has Come to Stay, page 125

Michelle Taggart

Michelle is a Principal Security Engineer at the Federal Reserve Bank of Boston, where she's responsible for planning and implementation of security solutions for the Federal Reserve System. Her IT career encompasses 16 years of varying cybersecurity roles, including digital forensics, vulnerability management, network and perimeter security, physical security, and governance, risk, and compliance. She also holds multiple industry certifications from (ISC)², ISACA, CSA, CompTIA, vendor-specific cloud certifications and a bachelor's degree from Drexel University. She is currently pursuing a master's degree in Cybersecurity at Norwich University. Being a first-generation college graduate, first-generation immigrant, and a mom of two amazing multiracial kids has inspired her to mentor and volunteer for various organizations that advocate for underrepresented groups' elevation in the cybersecurity space.

Opinions expressed in this contribution are solely of the contributor and do not express the views or opinions of the Federal Reserve.

Cloud Security: A 5,000 Mile View from the Top, page 128

Mike Mackintosh

Mike Mackintosh has served and led several security teams, most recently at Snap Inc. where he focused on security automation and hardening in addition to many other things. Before working at Snap Inc., Mike managed the security program at Shutterstock, overseeing application, infrastructure, and corporate security as well as contributing to the security of the startup Signal Sciences, helping the company earn its first production deployment. Mike has worked extensively on application security, DevOps, and security tooling as well as advising several startups on product roadmaps and helping them bake security into the company culture.

Balancing the Risk and Productivity of Browser Extensions, page 130

Ming Chow

Ming Chow is an Associate Teaching Professor at the Tufts University Department of Computer Science. His areas of interest are web and mobile security and computer science education. Ming has spoken at numerous organizations and conferences, including the HTCIA, OWASP, InfoSec World, Design Automation Conference (DAC), DEF CON, Intel, SOURCE, HOPE, Bsides, and ACM SIGCSE. He has served as a mentor to a BSides Las Vegas Proving Ground track speaker since 2014, a track focused on helping new speakers in the information security and hacker communities acclimate to public speaking. Ming was named the 2016 Henry and Madeline Fischer Award recipient at Tufts, awarded annually to a faculty member of the School of Engineering judged by graduating seniors of the School of Engineering to be "Engineering's Teacher of the Year." He was named the 2017 Lerman-Neubauer Prize for Outstanding Teaching and Advising recipient at Tufts, awarded annually to a faculty member who has had a profound intellectual impact on their students, both inside and outside the classroom.

Technical Project Ideas Towards Learning Web Application Security, page 132

Mitchell Parker

Mitchell Parker, MBA, CISSP, is the CISO at IU Health. He is responsible for providing policy and governance oversight and research, third-party vendor guidance, proactive vulnerability research and threat modeling services, payment card and financial systems security, and security research to IU Health and the IU School of Medicine. Mitch also actively researches and publishes in the academic community. He is an adjunct lecturer in Health Informatics at Indiana University–Purdue University Indianapolis (IUPUI), and also guest lectures at multiple universities, including IUPUI, Purdue, and the IU Kelley School of Business. He has also published peer-reviewed papers with collaborators across the world. Previous to his move to Indiana, Mitch was an Adjunct Professor in the Information Technology and Cyber Security (ITACS) program at the Fox School of Business at Temple University, where he taught MIS5903, the cybersecurity capstone course. Mitch also is a prolific presenter, having presented at Black Hat, DEFCON Recon and Biohacking Villages, IEEE TechIgnite, the national HIMSS conference multiple times, the HIMSS Security Forum, multiple ISMG Healthcare conferences, multiple regional HIMSS conferences, Becker's IT+Revenue Cycle conference, and numerous other regional and national conferences.

Monitoring: You Can't Defend Against What You Don't See, page 134

Najla Lindsay

Najla Lindsay is a forensics enthusiast, also known as Your Favorite #ScientistToHacker who has taken on the journey of transitioning to information security. She is a lab technician turned ICS/OT novice. She has spoken at several conferences and volunteers with the BioHacking Village. She is passionate about sharing resources and consistently growing her knowledge and skills. She loves wine, food, and traveling. You can find her on Twitter @ForSci_Q.

Documentation Matters, page 136

Naomi Buckwalter

Naomi Buckwalter, CISSP CISM, is the Director of Informa-tion Security and IT at Beam Technologies. She has over 20 years' experience in IT and security and has held roles in soft-ware engineering, security architecture, security engineering, and security leadership. As a cybersecurity career adviser and mentor for people around the world, her passion is helping people, particu-larly women, get into cybersecurity. Naomi volunteers with Philly Tech Sis-tas, a Philadelphia-based nonprofit helping women of color prepare for a career in IT and tech. Naomi has two master's degrees from Villanova Uni-versity and a Bachelor of Engineering from Stevens Institute of Technology. In her spare time, Naomi plays volleyball and stays active as the mother of two boys.

The Dirty Truth Behind Breaking into Cybersecurity, page 137

Nathan Chung

Nathan Chung is a cloud security architecture specialist with more than 20 years of experience in IT and cybersecurity. He is an advocate for women in cyber and neurodiversity. He serves on multiple boards, including WiCyS (Women in Cybersecurity) Colorado, IGNITE Worldwide, and Spark Mindset. In addition, he volunteers on more than 12 committees and groups. He is also the host of the NeuroSec podcast.

Cloud Security, page 139

Nick Gordon

Nick Gordon is an engineering manager on the Security Engineering team at Marqeta, and before that was a devel-oper on the Identity team at WeWork.

Empathy and Change, page 141

Nicole Dorsett

Nicole enjoyed over two decades of administrative experience for large corporations before finding a niche in IT It was in 2011, not long after earning a Bachelor's degree from Boston University, when she started to plot the pivot from clerical into a more dynamic career. Thanks to her parents introducing her to computers and gaming at an early age, her awe of technology remained. She returned to school and quickly found herself passionate about Information Security. After graduating cum laude from West L.A. College in her hometown, with an A.S. degree in Computer Network and Security Management, she was laser-focused on the future. Starting out as an InfoSec Analyst and Security Monitoring Administrator heightened her enthusiasm for learning and knowledge-sharing all things cybersecurity. Grateful for every opportunity, she remains a firm believer that iron sharpens iron—eager to volunteer and pay it forward.

Information Security Ever After, page 143

Patrick Schiess

Patrick Schiess is incredibly passionate about technology and loves having fun while learning new things. He started coding at age 11 and has been solving problems through code his entire professional career. His roots are from the Midwest US; he was born in a small town in rural Kentucky and eventually moved to Indiana, where he attended Purdue University. During his time at Purdue, he was involved in various musical and visual arts organizations, including the Purdue Jazz Band, Carolina Crown Drum and Bugle Corps, and Purdue Latin and Ballroom Dance Team. He met his wife through ballroom dance and they now live in Texas, where she is a radiologist and he is a technology professional in internet security/the high-tech industry.

Don't Check It In!, page 145

Phil Swaim

With 10 years as an information security and IT professional, Phil has worked in a variety of roles, including engineer, consultant, analyst, incident responder, and department leader. Since its founding, Phil has also been a key organizer for an annual security/hacker conference in Indianapolis, CircleCityCon. He enjoys playing video games, cooking, cosplaying, and tinkering in his lab.

Threat Modeling for SIEM Alerts, page 147

Priscilla Li

Priscilla Li is Security Engineering Manager at Cloudflare and an experienced cybersecurity professional who remains curious about all things security. She brings a wealth of experience in managing security-related projects, building security infrastructure, and incident response.

Security Incident Response and Career Longevity, page 149

Quiessence Phillips

Quiessence Phillips is a transformational leader, whose strategies and execution have helped build impactful and innovative teams in the cybersecurity industry. With over 12 years of experience spanning the private and public sector, she brings a wealth of knowledge and experience to her work. She also brings her experience and unique teaching style to a large body of students through her role as an adjunct professor at New York University.

Quiessence's leadership has yielded a first-of-its-kind centralized threat management program for a municipality—the City of New York, serving over 100 agencies, entities, and organizations. She currently holds the position of Deputy CISO for the City of New York and Head of Threat Management for New York City Cyber Command. Her teams span across Security Operations, Computer Emergency Response, Cyber Threat Intelligence, and Counter Threat Automation. Quiessence has been recognized as "Best of New York" by City Tech Foundation, published in *Women Know Cyber: 100 Fascinating Females Fighting Cybercrime*, and was awarded Security Team of the Year for the public sector by FireEye. For more information about her, visit *https://itsquiessence.com*.

Incident Management, page 151

Rob Newby

Rob Newby is the CEO of Procordr, a cybersecurity software startup based in the UK. He is a recovering CISO and previously worked as the Lead on large enterprise security transformation programs.

Structure over Chaos, page 153

Rushi Purohit

Rushi Purohit (*rpurohit@mitre.org*) is a Senior Cybersecurity Engineer at The MITRE Corporation (MITRE) with about six years of experience in secure code review, vulnerability analysis/management, threat modeling, software security research, training, and mentoring. Rushi is the technical lead for CWE Top 25 and CWE Mapping Guidance efforts and has been supporting the CWE project for the past three years. Rushi enjoys working on CWE and other technical and nontechnical projects that require diverse collaboration across communities.

CWE Top 25 Most Dangerous Software Weaknesses, page 155

Saju Thomas Paul

Saju Thomas Paul heads the threat hunting service within Atos IT Solutions and Service with a specialty in network hunting, malware analysis, user behavior analytics, and incident response, and manages a specialized team to deliver this service. For over 10 years Saju has been delivering and supporting niche clients across Asia, the Middle East, and North America.

Saju was previously a practice manager for professional services and was the architect for various compliance and regulatory requirements across multiple regions using managed detection and response. He has been contributing to the cyber industry through blogs and forums and at various technical summits.

Threat Hunting Based on Machine Learning, page 157

Sallie Newton

Sallie Newton is a Senior Product Security Engineer, Security Researcher at Intel Corporation. She holds several leading industry certifications, including the Certified Secure Software Lifecycle Professional (CSSLP) and the Certified Information Systems Security Professional (CISSP). As a former Product Security Incident Response Team (PSIRT) Lead, Sallie prioritizes amplifying the value add that security-minded developers and technologists bring to the product development life cycle. She has more than three decades of experience spanning compliance, business continuity, IT security program development, and Security Education, Training, and Awareness (SETA) program development and management, as well as serving in the role of virtual CISO for Fortune 500 companies.

Get In Where You Fit In, page 159

Sam Denard

Sam Denard, PhD, is a mechanical engineer trained at MIT, Stanford, and Texas Tech University. He has spent much of his professional career engineering software. For 25 years, he was an independent consultant with Empirical Products and Services (www.empiricalproducts.com). In addition, he has been employed in the consumer, nuclear energy, petroleum, and space exploration industries. Currently, he is a Senior Security Engineer with Fortify, a MicroFocus company.

Look Inside and See What Can Be, page 161

Sasha Rosenbaum

Sasha is a Sr. Manager of the Managed OpenShift Black Belt team at Red Hat, where she is helping enterprise customers successfully migrate to Managed OpenShift on customers' favorite public cloud. In her career, Sasha has worked in development, operations, consulting, and customer success. Sasha is an organizer of DevOpsDays Chicago, a chair of DeliveryConf, and the author of *Serverless Computing in Azure with .NET*.

DevOps for InfoSec Professionals, page 164

Shinesa Cambric

Shinesa Cambric (CISSP, CISA, CIAM, CDPSE), is an IT Security and Identity Architect with strategic expertise in the technical design of application, on-prem, and cloud security. Her experience includes architecting identity integration with cloud-based platforms, developing tools and strategies for business-critical ERP systems, building insider threat programs, and providing unique subject matter expertise on the intersection of governance, risk, and compliance with security and application development. She currently serves as a member of the operational team for the nonprofit group CloudGirls (cloudgirls.org), as an advisor for SecureWorld Dallas, and as training lead for the Dallas chapter of Women's Society of Cyberjutsu. Shinesa is an active member of several other organizations, including ISACA, (ISC)², AnitaB, Women in Cyber Security (WiCyS), the Information Systems Security Association (ISSA), the International Association of Privacy Professionals (IAPP), the Women's Cyber Security Society, the Executive Women's Forum, and the Identity Management Institute.

Get Familiar with R&R (Risk and Resilience), page 167

Siggi Bjarnason

Siggi was born in Reykjavik, Iceland during an era when there was more science fiction than fact. He got his first computer in the early 80s when only a teen and was online a few years later, about a decade before the invention of the web browser. Siggi went to Tacoma, WA to study computer engineering and earned a bachelor of science degree in 1994. 30 years later, he is still in the Seattle area. His career included a 13-year stint at Microsoft starting in 1995, and he is now Principle Cybersecurity Engineering at T-Mobile, USA Inc.

Password Management, page 169
Vulnerability Management, page 173

Stacey Champagne

Stacey believes that cybersecurity careers are a means to disrupt the inequity of wealth and power in society. As the Founder and CEO of Hacker in Heels, she attracts, advances, and advocates for women in cybersecurity through her membership community and programs. She is an active practitioner herself with specialized expertise in insider risk, and continues to lead in the field as the Information Security Program Manager for Compass, a modern real estate technology platform. Stacey holds multiple certifications, including Security+, Certified Forensic Computer Examiner (CFCE), and Insider Threat Program Manager (ITPM).

She earned her MS in Security and Resilience Studies with a focus on Cybersecurity Policy from Northeastern University, and a graduate certificate in Cybercrime Investigation and Cybersecurity from Boston University.

Reduce Insider Risk Through Employee Empowerment, page 175

Steven Becker

Steven Becker started his IT career on the help desk in 2005 and quickly began moving to sysadmin and netadmin roles, while increasing his focus on information security. He has accumulated many technical, security, and privacy certifications, and began working with CompTIA as a Subject Matter Expert to help better shape the future of IT and security professionals in 2017. He lives in the New York metro area with his wife and daughter, where he enjoys cooking, talking about wine, and golfing, among other hobbies.

Fitting Certifications into Your Career Path, page 178
Phishing Reporting Is the Best Detection, page 180

Steve Taylor

Steve Taylor is a Cloud Solution Architect at Microsoft, helping customers succeed with their security and identity in the cloud. He has over 15 years of experience in IT, from being a communications officer in the US Air Force to multiple customer-facing roles within Microsoft. He enjoys leveraging PowerShell to automate processes, analyze data, and secure systems.

Know Your Data, page 182

Tarah Wheeler

Tarah Wheeler is a Cyber Project Fellow at the Belfer Center for Science and International Affairs at Harvard University's Kennedy School of Government. She is an International Security Fellow at New America, leading a new international cybersecurity capacity building project with the Hewlett Foundation's Cyber Initiative and a US/UK Fulbright Scholar in Cyber Security for the 2020/2021 year. She is an Electronic Frontier Foundation advisory board member, an inaugural contributing cybersecurity expert for *The Washington Post*, and a *Foreign Policy* contributor on cyber warfare. She has appeared on Bloomberg Asia on US–China trade and cybersecurity. She is the author of the best-selling *Women in Tech: Take Your Career to the Next Level with Practical Advice and Inspiring Stories*. She is an information security researcher, political scientist in the area of international conflict, author, and poker player. She has spoken on information security at the European Union, at the Malaysian Securities Commission, the OECD, FTC, at universities such as Stanford, American, West Point, and Oxford, and at multiple governmental and industry conferences. Reach her at @tarah (*http://twit ter.com/tarah*).

Some Thoughts on PKI, page 188

Tim Maliyil

Tim Maliyil is a software engineer and the CEO of AlertBoot Cybersecurity, a global endpoint and file encryption services firm. Maliyil started his career in information security in 1999 when he joined Netegrity, a successful authentication and identity management software company. He was responsible for deploying the Netegrity software to enterprises around the world. With those experiences, along with being an enthusiastic engineer, Maliyil started several SaaS companies to foster his love of technology, business, and information security.

Don't Let the Cybersecurity Talent Shortage Leave Your Firm Vulnerable, page 184

Tkay Rice

Tkay Rice is an IT professional with seven years in the IT industry. She has had roles as a quality assurance software tester, security engineer, and a technical trainer. She has bachelor's and master's degrees in Cybersecurity and Assurance. What she enjoys most about working in IT is there is an abundant amount of information that is exposable and far too much to learn to get bored. During her personal time, she enjoys traveling, hiking, and spending time with friends and family.

Comfortable Versus Confident, page 186

Travis F. Felder

Travis Felder is a Security Consultant at Amazon Web Services and enjoys every opportunity to pioneer challenging security solutions that support meaningful customer initiatives and positive business outcomes. He has spent the majority of his cybersecurity career gaining experiences in areas such as application security, cloud security, and cybersecurity architecture. He holds a Master of Science degree in Cybersecurity and Information Assurance from Western Governors University, as well as a Bachelor of Science degree in Computer Engineering from Florida International University.

What Is a Security Champion?, page 190

Trevor Bryant

Trevor Bryant is an information technology expert specializing in the Risk Management Framework. He has championed, architected, and implemented CI/CD and secured automated provisioning frameworks and other modernized federal agency initiatives. He translates federal policy into technical implementations while also contributing to those policies. Being involved in both the DevOps and InfoSec communities, he emphasizes that security practices are usable through cost-effective, risk-based actions.

Risk Management in Information Security, page 193

Unique Glover

Unique Glover is a Technical Director in Microsoft's Modern Work and Security division, where he aims to help companies realize success in their digital transformation journey. Unique's 20-year career in IT spans several industry verticals with companies like UnitedHealth Group, EY, NCR, and Intercontinental Hotel Group (IHG). Unique specializes in identity and access management and has a background and passion for systems engineering, security architecture design, and cloud security. He is an advocate for increasing diverse representation in the information technology field and regularly volunteers time to mentor and educate on STEM career paths.

Risk, 2FA, MFA, It's All Just Authentication! Isn't It?, page 195

Valentina Palacin

Valentina Palacin, author of *Practical Threat Intelligence and Data-Driven Threat Hunting* and currently Threat Operations Lead at Marqeta, specializes in tracking APTs worldwide and using the ATT&CK framework to analyze their tools, tactics, and techniques. She is a self-taught developer and Threat Hunter with a degree in Translation and Interpretation from the Universidad de Málaga (UMA), and a Cyber Security Diploma from the Universidad Tecnológica Nacional (UTN). In her free time she helps coordinate the Blue-Space (@bluespacesec) and Open Threat Research (@OTR_Community) security communities.

Things I Wish I Knew Before Getting into Cybersecurity, page 197

Vanessa Redman

Vanessa Redman is a Cyber Scenario Developer and Strategy Consultant in Las Vegas, Nevada. She has proudly been playing with computers since getting a used Commodore VIC-20 in the late 1980s and loves learning about new things. Before working on scenarios to better train security teams, Vanessa worked as a Red Team Tech Lead, and has taught lessons on a variety of cybersecurity topics, including vulnerability management, adversary tactics, and threat intelligence. She loves playing the devil's advocate and is always looking for assumptions to disprove. She is currently studying Algorithmic and Behavioral Game Theory for use in Cyber Strategy (both offensive and defensive) and has presented her findings so far at conferences for BSidesLV, The Diana Initiative, Women's Society of Cyberjutsu (WSC), and Women in Cybersecurity (WiCyS). You can follow her on Twitter at @RedmanCyber.

Research Is Not Just for Paper Writing, page 199

Wayne A. Howell Jr.

Wayne A. Howell Jr. has over 15 years' experience in cybersecurity, network security, software development, risk management, compliance, and governance. His responsibilities include expertise in building strong cybersecurity programs and product security. Wayne is a member of the Bowie State University Computer Technology External Advisory Board, focusing on steering curriculum that meets the current demands of today's market. He is a philanthropist and serves as Vice President of Sow Good Project, Inc., a 501(c)3.

The Security Practitioner, page 201

Xena Olsen

Xena Olsen is a senior cybersecurity analyst for a Fortune 500 company. Xena is a graduate of SANS Women's Academy with eight GIAC certifications, has an MBA in Information Technology Management, and is a doctoral student in Cybersecurity at Marymount University.

Threat Intelligence in Two Steps, page 203

Yasmin Schlegel

 Yasmin Schlegel has over 20 years of experience in the federal government and private sectors in various intelligence analysis, systems engineering, cybersecurity, risk management, and compliance roles. She is an Army veteran and currently resides in Cincinnati, Ohio with her 10-year-old son Connor. Today, she works as a Principal GRC Analyst and can be reached on *LinkedIn* *(https://oreil.ly/HtvpV)*.

Maintaining Compliance and Information Security with Blue Team Assistance, page 205

Index

A

abusive relationships, stalkerware and, 117-118

access control, ethical data access, 61

Agile Manifesto, 50-52

Agile methodology
    for career path, 88-89
    Security Champions in, 190-192

AIDS_Trojan ransomware (Aids Info Disk), 46

alert fatigue, 84-85

alerts, threat modeling, 147-148

Amazon S3, 132

Amazon Web Services (AWS), 139

anonymity, importance of, 123-124

application password security, 145-146

asking questions, 2, 11, 23, 167

asset management, 15-16, 173

ATT&CK framework, 157-158

attackers
    advantage over cybersecurity professionals, 68
    hackers versus, 33
    internal threats, 40-41
    ransomware, 46-47
    threat hunting with machine learning, 157-158
    threat intelligence, 203-204

audience for presentations, 21-22

authentication, risk profiling and, 195-196

automation in DevOps, 165-166

availability, importance of, 71-72

AWS (Amazon Web Services), 139

B

balance in career, 109

baselines, establishing, 65-66

behavioral approach to information security, 25-26

blocker ransomware, 47

blogs
    with web application framework, 133
    in WordPress, 133

blue team, compliance management and, 205-206

browser extensions, 130-131

burnout, 34, 149-150

business needs
    availability and, 71
    importance of, 17-18
    people-focused security, 73-74
    risk management and, 53-54, 119-120, 167-168, 201-202

C

C-level executives, training in cybersecurity, 185

career path
  Agile methodology applied to, 88-89
  balance in, 109
  burnout, risk of, 34, 149-150
  certifications, 105-106, 178-179
  control of, 11-12
  entry-level positions, 137-138
  growth in, 109-110
  policy writing, 159-160
  research, importance of, 199-200
  security training for existing team, 184-185
  skills needed for, 29-30
  soft skills, 92-93
  switching careers, 110, 159
  tips for success, 143-144, 197-198
  traits needed for, 77-78
  unconventional, 89-89
  upskilling, 34-35

CAs (certificate authorities), 188
CASB (cloud access security broker), 128
certificate databases, 188
certificate stores, 188
certifications, 105-106, 140, 178-179
change management, 141-142
chaos, structure versus, 153-154
CI/CD (continuous integration and continuous delivery), 165-166
CISA certification, 179
Cisco certification, 179
CISM certification, 179
CISSP certification, 179
cloud access security broker (CASB), 128
cloud security, 62-64, 127
  certifications for, 140
  challenges, 63-64
  high-level view, 128-129
  isolation zones, 100-102

shared responsibility model, 48-49, 62-63
  vulnerabilities in cloud services, 139-140
  web application security, 59
cloud security agreement (CSA), 128
cloud security posture management solution (CSPM), 129
cluster security, 126
CND (computer network defense), 3
cognitive bias, 25-26
comfort, confidence versus, 186-187
Common Vulnerabilities and Exposures (CVEs), 156, 202
Common Vulnerability Scoring System (CVSS) scores, 156
Common Weakness Enumeration (CWE), 155-156, 202
communication
  of business needs, 17-18
  in change management, 141-142
  confidence versus comfort, 186-187
  of disaster recovery plans, 9-10
  fact versus fiction, 195-196
  importance of, 12
  listening and empathy in, 92-93
  metrics in presentations, 21-22
  in problem-solving, 19-20
  in risk management, 23-24, 32
communication skills
  importance of, 1-2, 29
  improving, 111-112
community, learning within, 1
compassion, importance of, 30
compliance
  blue team and, 205-206
  requirements, 159
CompTIA certification, 178
Computer Security Resource Center (CSRC), 86
confidence, comfort versus, 186-187

configuration management, 174

container security, 126

containment, 4-5, 151-152

continuous learning

importance of, 1-2, 29-30, 77

official sources, 36-37

patience in, 36-37

steps in, 11-12

in unknown unknowns, 183

upskilling, 34-35

web application security projects,
132-133

control sets, 153

cost of certifications, 105-106

CRISC certification, 179

cryptographic algorithms, 189

CSA (cloud security agreement), 128

CSPM (cloud security posture management solution), 129

CSRC (Computer Security Resource Center), 86

culture of DevOps, 164-165

customer notifications in incident
response, 81-83

CVEs (Common Vulnerabilities and
Exposures), 156, 202

CVSS (Common Vulnerability Scoring
System) scores, 156

CWE (Common Weakness Enumeration),
155-156, 202

cyber hygiene, 94-95

D

data at rest

privacy and, 14

security implications, 60

data in transit

privacy and, 14

security implications, 60

data in use, security implications, 60

data knowns/unknowns, 182-183

Data plane, interaction with Identity and
Privileges planes, 6-8

demilitarized zone (DMZ), 100-102

dependencies in Open Source Software
(OSS), 80

detection engineers, 149

device management for IoT (Internet of
Things), 107-108

DevOps, 50-52

automation, 165-166

culture of, 164-165

resources for information, 166

security in, 69-70

DevSecOps

continuous security, 125-127

evolution of, 69-70

digital forensics, 103-104

disaster recovery plans, 9-10

DMZ (demilitarized zone), 100-102

documentation

in change management, 142

importance of, 136

E

email

encryption, 189

phishing, 96-97, 171-172, 180-181

in threat intelligence, 204

empathy, importance of, 30, 92-93

employees

as stakeholders, 160

insider risk, mitigating, 175-177

security training for, 184-185

encryption algorithms, 189

encryptor ransomware, 46

entry-level cybersecurity positions,
137-138

ethical data access, 61

ethical hacking, 123-124

experience gap, overcoming, 184-185

F

failures, learning from, 78, 90-91
fake ransomware, 46
flexibility, importance of, 12
forensics, 103-104
frameworks
    for incident response, 151-152
    structure versus chaos, 153-154

G

gatekeepers for cybersecurity positions,
    105-106, 137-138

H

hackers
    attackers versus, 33
    ethics/morality of, 123-124
    legal issues, 44-45
    VDPs and, 33-34
hands-on learning, 2
health, personal availability and, 72
history of ransomware, 46
human-centered information security,
    25-26
hybrid cloud services, 63
hygiene in information security, 94-95
hypothetical syllogism, 8

I

IaaS (infrastructure as a service) in shared
    responsibility model, 63
IAM (identity and access management),
    user experience and, 42-43
identities, defined, 42
Identity plane, interaction with Data and
    Privileges planes, 6-8
imposter syndrome, overcoming, 144, 186
improving communication skills, 111-112
improvisational comedy as problem-
    solving approach, 19-20
incident response

alert fatigue, 84-85
burnout, avoiding, 149-150
customer notifications and, 81-83
defining normal, 65-66
digital forensics and, 103-104
patience in, 27-28
psychology of, 121-122
quantifying via frameworks, 151-152
tunnel vision in, 28
information security, defined, 205
internal incidents, 81
internal threats, 40-41, 175-177
internal zones, 100-102
IoT (Internet of Things), device manage-
    ment, 107-108
isolation zones, 100-102

K

key archival servers, 189
known knowns and unknowns, 182-183

L

Lean, 52
learning (see continuous learning)
legal issues, 44-45
liability in risk management, 23-24
licensing Open Source Software (OSS),
    79-80
Linux, security of, 55-56
listening, importance of, 92-93
logging
    importance of, 134-135
    password security and, 145-146

M

machine learning, threat hunting with,
    157-158
mandates in change management, 141
mergers & acquisitions, asset management
    in, 16
metrics in presentations, 21-22

misconfiguration of cloud resources, 140

mistakes, learning from, 78, 90-91

monitoring, importance of, 134-135

morality of hacking, 123-124

multilayered security approach, 94-95

N

NCCoE (National Cybersecurity Center of Excellence), 87

network engineers, training in cybersecurity, 185

NIST (National Institute of Standards and Technology), 86-87

NIST Cybersecurity Framework, 154

noise, alert fatigue and, 84-85

normal, defining, 65-66

note taking, importance of, 200

NVD (National Vulnerability Database), 87, 156

O

official sources for continuous learning, 36-37

OODA (Observe-Orient-Decide-Act) loop, 3-5

operating systems, Linux, 55-56

organizational needs (see business needs)

OSCP certification, 179

OSS (Open Source Software), licensing, 79-80

P

PaaS (platform as a service) in shared responsibility model, 63

panic, avoiding, 121

parental control software, stalkerware versus, 117

passion for information security, 77

password managers, 169-170

password security, 145-146, 169-170

patience

in continuous learning, 36-37

in incident response, 27-28

paying in ransomware attacks, 47

PC_Cyborg ransomware, 46

penetration tests

legal issues and, 44-45

steps in, 75-76

people-focused security, 73-74, 203

performance expectations in cybersecurity, 67-68

perimeter-based model, 48

personal availability, health and, 72

personal devices/networks, securing, 88-89

PGP (Pretty Good Privacy), 189

phishing, 96-97, 171-172, 180-181

PIR (post-incident review), 83

PKI (public key infrastructure), 188-189

planning

for disaster recovery, 9-10

security programs, 98-99

PMP certification, 179

policy writing, 159-160

post-incident review (PIR), 83

presentations, knowing audience, 21-22

prioritizing in asset management, 15-16

privacy in third-party environments, 13-14

private cloud services, 63

Privileges plane, interaction with Data and Identity planes, 6-8

proactive security approaches, reactive approaches versus, 197-198, 202

problem-solving, 19-20, 38-39

projects

learning web application security, 132-133

problem-solving approaches, 19-20

psychology of incident response, 121-122

public cloud services, 63

public key infrastructure (PKI), 188-189

public zones, 100-102

publishing disaster recovery plans, 9

Q

quantifying incident response, 151-152

questions, asking, 2, 11, 23, 167

R

ransomware
    history of, 46
    large-scale attacks, 47
    paying in attacks, 47
    types of, 46-47

RAs (registration authorities), 188

reactive security approaches, proactive
    approaches versus, 197-198, 202

reconnaissance in penetration tests, 75

remembered data in digital forensics,
    103-104

reporting phishing attempts, 180-181

reports on penetration tests, 76

research, importance of, 199-200

resilience, risk management and, 167-168

resources for information, 86-87, 166

risk management, 193-194
    business needs and, 53-54, 119-120,
        167-168, 201-202
    in career path, 78
    in cloud services, 59
    communication in, 23-24, 32
    cyber hygiene, 94-95
    in DevSecOps, 70
    insider threats, 40-41, 175-177
    people-focused security, 73-74
    role of, 31-32

risk profiling, authentication and, 195-196

S

S/MIME (Secure/Multipurpose Internet
    Mail Extensions), 189

SaaS (software as a service)

privacy and, 13-14
    in shared responsibility model, 63

SBOM (software bill of materials), 79-80

scanning tools, 114

schism in cybersecurity, 67-68

security awareness programs, 20

Security Champions, 190-192

Security Chaos Engineering, 90-91

Security Development Lifecycle, 59

Security Incident Response Team (SIRT),
    149

security principles, 57-58

security programs, developing, 98-99

self-regulation in incident response,
    121-122

serverless computing, security principles
    for, 57-58

shared responsibility model, 48-49, 62-63

sharing progress, 136

shortage of cybersecurity professionals,
    137

SIRT (Security Incident Response Team),
    149

social engineering, 115-116
    (see also phishing)

soft skills
    in change management, 141-142
    importance of, 92-93

software bill of materials (SBOM), 79-80

software development, 59
    delivery life cycle, 165-166
    DevSecOps in, 125-127
    evolution of DevSecOps, 69-70
    security tools in, 201

software engineers, training in cybersecur-
    ity, 184-185

SolarWinds hack, 1

solving problems, 19-20, 38-39

source code, password management and,
    145-146

spyware, stalkerware versus, 117

SSL/TLS certificates, 189
stakeholders
    employees as, 160
    self-regulation in incident response,
        121-122
    threat intelligence requirements, 204
stalkerware, 117-118
static analysis, 161-163
static websites, building, 132
stealer ransomware, 47
strong passwords, 169-170
structure, chaos versus, 153-154
Swartz, Aaron, 123
switching careers, 110, 159

T

team members (see employees)
telecommunications in problem-solving
    approaches, 19
testing disaster recovery plans, 10
third-party environments, privacy in,
    13-14
threat hunting with machine learning,
    157-158
threat intelligence, 203-204
threat mitigation, security principles for,
    57-58
threat models, 40-41
    for alerts, 147-148
    Security Champions and, 191
tools
    in problem-solving, 38-39
    security in software development, 201
triage analysts, 149
TTPs (tactics, techniques, and proce-
    dures), 157-158
tunnel vision
    in incident response, 28
    in penetration tests, 76

U

unconventional career paths, 89-89
unknown unknowns, 183
updating disaster recovery plans, 10
upskilling, 34-35
user data
    ethical access, 61
    in third-party environments, 13-14
user experience in IAM, 42-43

V

VDPs (vulnerability disclosure policies),
    33-34
vendors, privacy and, 13-14
visualization in incident response, 152
VM (vulnerability management), 113-114,
    173-174
vulnerabilities
    in cloud computing, 139-140
    CWE (Common Weakness Enumera-
        tion), 155-156
    in DevSecOps, 70
    NVD (National Vulnerability Data-
        base), 87
    penetration tests for, 75-76
    weaknesses versus, 202
vulnerability disclosure policies (VDPs),
    33-34
vulnerability management (VM), 113-114,
    173-174

W

weaknesses, vulnerabilities versus, 202
web application frameworks, 133
web application security, 59
    browser extensions, 130-131
    projects for learning, 132-133
web server authentication/encryption, 189
WordPress blogs, 133

About the Editor

Christina Morillo

Christina Morillo is an information security, "cybersecurity," and technology leader with an extensive background in enterprise security, identity and access management, security and IT operations, and cloud. In her current role, she leads the cloud security assessment service for Microsoft Cloud Services, including Azure Active Directory and Microsoft 365. As a strategic thinker who thrives on solving complex problems, her experience has taken her to companies such as Microsoft, Morgan Stanley, and Fitch Ratings.

By demystifying security and technology, she hopes to make security accessible, approachable, and digestible, with the overarching goal of keeping people and organizations safe and secure.

Lightning Source UK Ltd.
Milton Keynes UK
UKHW021259251021
392803UK00010B/42